VISUAL QUICKSTART GUIDE

Upgrading PCs

Bart Farkas
Jeff Govier

 Peachpit Press

Visual QuickStart Guide
Upgrading PCs
Bart Farkas
Jeff Govier

Peachpit Press
1249 Eighth Street
Berkeley, CA 94710
(510) 524-2178
(800) 283-9444
(510) 542-2221 (fax)

Find us on the World Wide Web at
www.peachpit.com

Peachpit Press is a division of Addison Wesley Longman

Editors: Simon Hayes and Corbin Collins
Copy editor: Colleen Paretty
Production coordinator: Amy Changar
Compositor: Lisa Brazieal
Cover design: The Visual Group
Indexer: Emily Glossbrenner

ISBN: 0-201-35422-5

9 8 7 6 5 4 3 2 1

Printed and bound in the United States of America

Dedication

For Robin and Cori, *amor vincit omnia.*

About the Authors

Bart G. Farkas has written more than 20 computer and video game books. He has also published numerous articles in Mac Home Journal and MacAddict magazine over the years. Bart lives with his wife, son, and two cats in Calgary, Canada.

Jeff Govier has worked in technical support, instruction, and programming (where he is currently stationed) for more than six years. He is the co-author of several computer books and is an experienced hardware technician. Jeff lives with his wife in Calgary, Canada.

Acknowledgments

Jeff: I would like to thank the following people for their contribution to the project. These folks gave their blood, sweat, tears, and time just for the thrill of seeing their names in the front of this book. Thanks to our hardware wranglers Steve Coutts and Leon Budlong. Thanks to Robin, my beautiful wife, and Bart, my almost-as-beautiful co-author. Finally, thank-you, Michael Goodwin for making this book better.

Bart: First and foremost I'd like to thank Jeff, whose staggering knowledge of PCs was instrumental in the writing of this book. I'd also like to thank the folks at Peachpit for their support and help. For Corbin Collins, Simon Hayes, and Marjorie Baer, a hearty thank you for all your help. Lastly, I'd like to thank Michael Goodwin, whose extensive knowledge of the inner workings of PCs helped to take this book to the next level.

TABLE OF CONTENTS

INTRODUCTION

Welcome to *Upgrading PCs: Visual QuickStart Guide!*

Not so many years ago, upgrading a PC practically required a doctorate in electrical engineering from M.I.T. Fortunately, times have changed, and upgrading your PC is not only much, much easier, but is now also very cost-effective in most cases.

Our goal for this book was to make the *fundamentals* of upgrading a PC easily accessible to anyone who owns one. After all, with so many new video cards, 3D accelerators, network cards, and even faster CPUs constantly hitting the market there's bound to be some part of their computer that users will want to upgrade from time to time. At the same time, we didn't want to include endless sections on everything under the sun. We wanted to create a slim, affordable guide to the basics of upgrading your PC—and nothing more. We hope we have succeeded.

You may look at portions of this book and see acronyms like IRQ and DMA bandied about and start to get cold feet, but not to worry. We're here to tell you that although you may occasionally have to dive into the unsavory world of jumpers and BIOS settings, the newer your machine is, the more those are things of the past. Indeed, *most* new hardware installations go very smoothly and require little extra effort on your part, other than to pop a new card into your computer and follow the steps laid out with the New Hardware Wizard in Windows 98.

But if your problems are more serious, this book can help with that as well, and you'll no doubt notice some references to procedures that may not apply to your situation. Basically, we hope you'll take as much or as little from this book as is necessary to get you upgraded and up and running as fast and with as little difficulty as possible.

We've broken the book down into sections that cover the various categories of upgrades, but we recommend that you read through Chapters 1 and 2 first to get the overall picture of what is needed before you go cracking open your computer case. Happy upgrading!

HARDWARE UPGRADING INTRODUCTION

1

Without a doubt, one of the most daunting tasks for the average computer owner is upgrading an aging machine's hardware. After all, when you take the case off your PC, the maze of wires, cards, and even the motherboard itself are truly intimidating sights. But upgrading your PC isn't nearly as difficult as many computer pundits would have you believe. You don't need a degree in computer science, a technical certificate, or even a crash course in ancient mysticism.

Although problems with resource conflicts, mismatched bus types, and dirty contacts are not uncommon, most of the difficulty in installing new hardware comes from configuring the software that makes it work rather than physically placing the new hardware. For the most part, upgrading your PC calls for a few basic rules and even fewer tools to successfully "operate" on your silicon workhorse.

This book is meant to be your guiding light, showing you how to make your PC better without taking ten years off your life. We've called on our combined 25 years of PC experience to create an easy-to-use upgrading book for people just like you. So, let's get to it.

Required Tools

As with any do-it-yourself project, gathering the correct tools for the job before you start will save you plenty of frustration and possibly even prevent damage to your computer's components. Fortunately, the homogenous design of PCs means you'll need only a short list of tools for most hardware upgrades as shown in **Figure 1.1**.

◆ A multi-bit screwdriver.

◆ Needle-nose pliers.

◆ Adequate lighting.

◆ Utility knife.

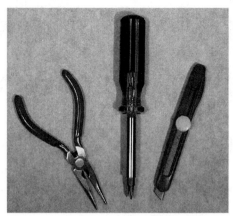

Figure 1.1 A comprehensive family portrait of the tools necessary for most PC hardware upgrades.

Usually, that's all you'll need to open a computer case, install a new adapter card or drive, and close the case back up again. It should take you very little time to become comfortable with the physical process of installing new components into your computer.

For a small number of computers on the market, you'll need more tools. Some computer cases, for example, open with special proprietary tools available only to elite technicians who work in the manufacturer's world. That's why we highly recommend you consider how easily a computer case can be removed when you buy a new system; make convenient accessibility a purchasing requirement.

Multi-bit screwdriver

Some manufacturers use different screw heads to attach case covers and pieces inside the case, so a multi-bit screwdriver allows you to adapt to whatever random combination of screws you may encounter. We recommend you find a multi-bit screwdriver with as many different kinds of bits as possible, including Phillips, Robertson, and flathead.

Is It Worth Upgrading?

With processor speeds doubling every 18 months (a phenomenon known as *Moore's Law*) and the price of computers tumbling faster than a figure skater with an inner ear infection, it may not always make sense to upgrade your PC. As a general rule of thumb, if your PC is more than two years old, you should probably look at simply buying a new machine if you can afford it. However, if you have an old machine and all you need is a little more RAM or a new hard drive, then an upgrade is probably your best bet. We like to follow the rule that if upgrading is going to cost you 60 to 70 percent of the price of a new computer, go for the new computer.

Figure 1.2 Needle-nose pliers are ideal for tackling loose serial/parallel port mounting posts.

Needle-nose pliers

Although the need for a screwdriver is fairly obvious (it is the single most important tool you'll be using), needle-nose pliers are also essential. They have 1,001 uses and can take care of everything from twisting off those screws for which no screwdriver seems to exist to turning the mounting posts that attach parallel and serial port connectors to the back of your computer case. These posts tend to loosen until eventually they come right out of their sockets. As far as we know, needle-nose pliers are the only force in the universe capable of efficiently reattaching these posts. **Figure 1.2** shows a typical pair of needle-nose pliers in action on some mounting posts.

Needle-nose pliers also make quick work of stubborn jumpers on motherboards and adapter cards, and they are indispensable for retrieving dropped screws or other small items that seem to have the habit of falling inside the computer case.

Proper lighting

Always work in a very brightly lit area. But even so, you'll need a flashlight to see into the depths of your computer case. We prefer flashlights that have an adjustable beam rather than a tightly focused beam; the latter can be a challenge to aim if all you need is a general light. Whatever the case, the extra illumination comes in handy for seeing jumper settings, confirming that pieces are connected properly, or finding dropped screws.

Recommended Tools

These tools aren't mandatory for upgrading PCs, but they will make your life a heck of a lot easier.

Computer hardware toolkits

Buying a computer hardware toolkit is certainly a good way to begin a tool collection. **Figure 1.3** shows a typical toolkit. They're available at just about every computer store that sells hardware. Many sport a puzzling array of implements that look capable of performing both brain surgery and Saturn V rocket repair. These special-purpose tools exist for almost any conceivable circumstance. A few examples:

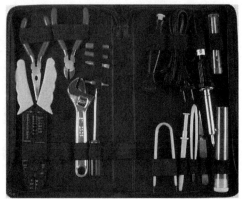

Figure 1.3 A typical computer hardware toolkit puts plenty of useful tools at your fingertips.

♦ **Retractable wire forceps** for picking up dropped screws or other small items inside a computer case.

♦ **A claw-like chip-puller** is handy for extracting computer chips from their sockets. PCs manufactured in the last four years feature CPUs mounted on sockets that require no tools for insertion or extraction. Only the oldest of 486-class PCs will require this item.

♦ **Six- and eight-point screwdrivers** are great for screws that no one outside the computer hardware industry has ever seen. (PC manufacturers are endlessly inventive when designing components.) These esoteric screwdrivers are only needed infrequently.

These kits are often very reasonably priced and usually include the multi-bit screwdriver and the needle-nose pliers you need anyway, while the rest of the items will impress almost anyone who hasn't read this chapter. Just make sure that what you need is in the toolkit, and don't spend a lot of extra money on implements you won't use much.

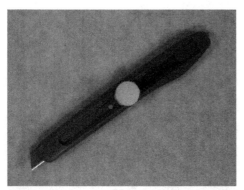

Figure 1.4 A utility knife is handy for slicing through packaging.

For less than $20 you should find a great kit with more tools than you'll ever need.

✔ Tip

■ Note that the multi-bit screwdriver in most toolkits has a handle that is not as large, easy to grip, or twist as screwdrivers you can buy separately. Since this is the most important tool you will use, make sure you have a one that is comfortable and convenient.

Most hobbyists would agree that the best tool that could come to market is a third hand. But because most of us will never have more than two hands, we'll have to settle for the following alternatives.

Utility knife

A utility knife (**Figure 1.4**) is irreplaceable for slicing through the shrink-wrap that invariably entombs store-bought items. CD-ROM cases, for example, are usually bound in notoriously impenetrable wrappers, and a sharp blade will save you some frustration.

Flashlights

Flashlights worn like a hat or mounted to a stand are great for illuminating a task requiring two hands. A reading lamp mounted on an adjustable arm is also acceptable.

Another excellent type of flashlight can be twisted like a snake, allowing the user to wrap it around a forearm. Personal preference is also important; most home centers and hardware stores carry a good variety of lighting options.

The old pen and paper

Last, keep a pen and paper handy. Solving hardware problems is often a matter of trial and error. Making notes about what you have tried already is a far more reliable way of keeping track of your progress than trying to remember everything. Also, when you change a hardware or software setting, noting the original state of your system can save you a lot of grief later. In the excitement to make things work, you may be tempted to skip taking notes; keeping a pen and paper around lessens the temptation and helps you work systematically.

Polaroid camera

Though a camera may seem an expensive convenience, it is definitely a lifesaver. Taking pictures of the inside of your system before you start any procedure can give you an excellent reference for reconnecting parts and pieces. Use the camera to take wide-angle shots, as well as close-up pictures of each component on which you are working. Having this instant reference if something goes wrong can save you heaps of trouble, so if you have an old Polaroid lying around the house, dust it off.

Compressed air

A can of compressed air (**Figure 1.5**) removes dust from the inside of your computer case. Although a little dust is normal, excessive buildup will ultimately interfere with heat dissipation and reduce the life of your components. Blow away dust whenever you see any on the inside of the computer case.

Figure 1.5 Compressed air quickly rids your computer case of dust.

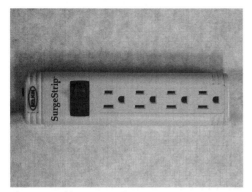

Figure 1.6 Tabletop power bar.

Recommended Workspace Provisions

Home PCs often live in offices, bedrooms, or dining rooms. But since these areas tend to be cluttered with papers and files, extra disks, and CD-ROMs, and empty plates and fast-food containers (in Bart's case), they are not really ideal environments for working on your system.

If you can't clear the area around your computer, try to find another nice, clear, well-lit tabletop or work area so you can put your tools and hardware parts down safely and keep them within easy reach.

The following items are nice to have:

◆ Tabletop power bar to give you access to multiple outlets in one location (**Figure 1.6**).

◆ Adjustable desk lamp.

◆ Plastic storage containers for extra screws, parts, and pieces.

◆ Anti-static mat. (Read more about static mats in the section "Static mats," later in this chapter.)

✔ Tips

■ A cluttered work area is probably the number-one cause of lost screws, so be vigilant. A clean, bare floor under your worktable makes it simple to find the pieces that can't resist the pull of gravity.

■ A wood desktop is much better than a metal surface because wood does not conduct (attract) electricity, which can damage your computer's components.

Beware Static Electricity

Every hardware manual warns about static electricity, and although the danger may seem small, it's worth taking precautions to ensure that you don't fry any of your components.

Static Electricity

Many forms of electricity can damage your computer. Obviously, lightning that strikes your house or even a fluctuating power source can cause major damage to your computer, but there's a far more sinister electricity source lurking nearby: static electricity.

A static electrical charge that you may be carrying (from, say, shuffling your feet on a carpet) may seem harmless to you, but it can be lethal to a computer chip. A typical static charge (you see a small, blue spark come off your finger or you hear a snapping sound) may deliver more than 10,000 volts!

How dangerous is it, actually? Well, in everyday use with your computer case on, it's a non-issue. But when you're actually touching logic boards, there's a little more need for concern. It's true that, nine times out of ten, you can pass along a static shock to your computer and do no damage. On the other hand, there is that tenth time... if you're unlucky you could fry your motherboard with a single static shock. No need to become obsessed with this, but it makes sense to be careful what you touch and stay grounded, both literally and emotionally.

Grounding

1. First, ground yourself with a static wristband connected to the power supply inside your computer before touching any other interior component, as shown in **Figure 1.7**.

Figure 1.7 Touch the power-supply box inside your computer case before and after you work on components.

Figure 1.8 Static wrist guards don't cost much and help ground you.

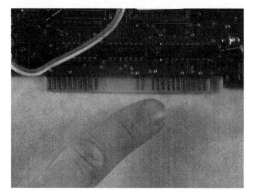

Figure 1.9 Whatever you do, stay away from the connectors on adapter cards. These areas are the most sensitive to static electricity.

If you don't ground yourself, every time you move away from the case and then return to continue work, make sure to touch the power-supply casing. By doing so, you dissipate any charge you may have generated while away from the machine.

2. Connect your computer to an electrical ground. To do that, use a length of wire or a spare anti-static wristband to connect any metal surface of your computer to another metal surface—good candidates are faucets and radiators.

✔ Tip

■ You can pick up disposable static bands (like the one shown in **Figure 1.8**) at most computer stores. For more on these wristbands, see Chapter 2.

Careful where you touch

Never handle adapter cards or printed circuit boards by their connector tabs (**Figure 1.9**). Whether or not you are carrying a charge, you may complete a circuit between the connector leads, which would allow a stored charge in the card to dissipate and damage the component. Handle printed circuit boards by their edges only.

Static mats

Extremists may want to go the whole nine yards and pick up a static mat to place under the computer case. The small investment is worthwhile. The mat is usually grounded to a power outlet and often comes with a static wristband that grounds you at the same time.

Some Hardware Terms

If the inside of a computer case is new territory for you, this section will familiarize you with certain terms used commonly in this book. Be sure to read through these before undertaking hardware upgrade projects. You can also refer to this book's Glossary.

Adapter cards

An adapter card is a printed circuit board that fits into an expansion slot inside your computer. Internal modems, network cards, and video cards are all examples of adapter cards. **Figure 1.10** shows four adapter cards with their connectors pointing down.

Motherboards

The motherboard is the main printed circuit board around which your computer system is built. The single largest component inside your computer case, the motherboard (shown removed from a computer case in **Figure 1.11**) is easy to identify even though it is often buried under cables and adapter cards at the bottom of the system.

The type of motherboard you have determines the kind of CPU you can use, how much memory you can add to your PC, how many adapter cards you can install at the same time, and most other aspects of your computer's configuration. They are sometimes referred to as main boards or system boards. **Figure 1.12** shows a motherboard inside the computer case.

Figure 1.10 These are some examples of adapter cards. The connectors are all pointing down.

Figure 1.11 A PC motherboard is the largest component in your system.

Figure 1.12 This PC motherboard is shown inside a computer.

Figure 1.13 An empty expansion slot on a motherboard waiting for an adapter card.

Figure 1.14 An adapter card fitting into a slot.

Expansion slots

An expansion slot is a connector on the motherboard that is designed to hold an adapter card (**Figure 1.13** shows empty expansion slots). Expansion slots are occasionally called bus slots because their type or classification is determined by the bus they attach to. There are a few different types of expansion slots and, as you might expect, you need to match the type of adapter card with the type of slot. Unless a cable is in the way, or won't reach, the location of the slot you choose doesn't matter as long as it matches the card you are installing.

Sliding a card into an expansion slot often requires more pushing, shoving, wiggling and cursing than you'd expect—but most cards will eventually fit into the slot on the motherboard (**Figure 1.14**). Once a board is properly seated, you can lock it into place with a single screw to the side of the case.

SOME HARDWARE TERMS

Central processing units (CPUs)

The microprocessor (CPU) inside your computer is packaged in a ceramic casing with connectors on one side. Depending on the type of CPU, it either fits into a socket on the motherboard, or mounts on a small board that fits in a slot on the motherboard.

Until the Intel Pentium II processor came along, all PC microprocessors used a socket; the most recent one is called socket 7. The Pentium II and Celeron processors use slot 1. Processors from other manufacturers, such as American Micro Devices and Cyrix, use a socket because Intel patented the slot connectors to prevent other CPU makers from following in their slot 1 footsteps. In **Figure 1.15** you can see a socket for an older CPU.

Figures 1.16 through **1.19** show CPU slots empty and full.

Figure 1.15 CPUs come in two modes: This is a CPU socket.

Figure 1.16 The CPU socket is empty.

Figure 1.17 The CPU socket is now full.

Figure 1.18 This CPU slot is empty.

Figure 1.19 This CPU slot is now full.

Kinds of Hardware Upgrades

We will not discuss any procedure that involves soldering, popping chips out of printed circuits, splicing power leads, or using a multimeter, so you won't have to go to technical school at night to keep up with us.

The upgrade projects in this book are organized into five areas:

◆ **Communication devices.** Network cards and internal modems.

◆ **Storage devices.** Hard-disk and CD-ROM drives.

◆ **Video devices.** 2-D/primary video cards, 3-D/secondary video cards, and multiple primary video cards running under Windows 98.

◆ **Sound devices.** Sound cards for ISA and PCI buses, plus USB speaker systems.

◆ **Core components.** The CPU, motherboard, and system memory (RAM).

Each section explains and illustrates the complete procedure for every installation, from setting up the hardware to configuring the software. After you've actually performed a few procedures, you will find that it is not a daunting task to pull off the cover of your computer to make changes or do upgrades.

Don't get us wrong—the inside of a PC is not somewhere to venture unprepared or on a whim. However, it is designed to allow relatively simple servicing and upgrading. And even the least technically inclined user should not shy away from trying his or her hand at some hardware upgrades and configuration tasks. For one thing, it can save you significant amounts of time—not to mention money that you'd otherwise pay to a professional.

First Things First

The following are very important steps you should take before you start upgrading your PC. Refer back to this part of the book early and often. Although these things may seem unnecessary when you're doing them, they can save you heaps of trouble later on. And although this list isn't something you *must* do before upgrading, we highly recommend it.

What to do before you get started

1. Read the printed and/or electronic instructions that accompany the hardware you want to install. There is often a Readme file on the CD-ROM or floppy disk that may have come with the hardware. The Readme may contain new information that was omitted in the printed material.

2. Write down your system information, including IRQs, DMAs, hard drive information, and system settings. You can find this information by clicking on the Start menu (in Windows 95 and 98) and then selecting Accessories > System Tools > System Information. This window is shown in **Figure 1.20**.

3. In Windows 95 and 98, you can also get the pertinent information from every piece of hardware in your computer by right-clicking on the My Computer icon on your desktop, selecting Properties, and then selecting the Device Manager tab, as shown in **Figure 1.21**.

Figure 1.20 Write down your pertinent system information from the MS Information utility.

Figure 1.21 Get all your current hardware information from the Device Manager.

4. Make sure you have a Windows Startup Disk, which you can use to reboot your machine if something goes wrong with your hard disk.

When you first installed Windows 95 or 98, you were offered a chance to create a Windows Startup disk. If you created one then, make sure you can find that disk now. If you didn't create one then or can't find it, you can create one at anytime: Put a blank floppy disk into your drive. Click on Start > Settings > Control Panel > Add/Remove Programs (Startup Disk tab), and click Create Disk. Keep it in a handy spot near your computer.

5. Put labels on any cables that you'll be disconnecting from the inside or outside of your computer case. This is an important step, because it's easy to lose track of which cable goes where once the cables have all been disconnected.

FIRST THINGS FIRST

GENERAL INSTALLATION GUIDE

2

As a rule, most hardware installation procedures follow the same pattern: open the computer case, plug in the hardware, test the installation, and put everything back together. The preparations for each procedure are also quite similar. This chapter outlines those preparations and the configuration considerations you should make before adding any hardware to your system. Please read this chapter *before* you begin any hardware procedure.

Precautions and Preparations

As the previous chapter stressed, prepare a convenient, well-lit workspace that allows you free access to your computer system. If you must move your computer to another location before opening it up, make sure that you also bring the grounding wire and wrist straps.

If you do not need to move your computer, then simply leave all the connections intact. Unplug it, and disconnect only those cables or wires that are attached to hardware items you are replacing or removing. In some rare cases, you'll need to remove some connectors to remove the case cover. If you plan to use a Polaroid or other camera, this is a good time to take close-up pictures of cables, boards, and other components before they are disassembled.

Anti-static

Run a ground wire from the computer's power supply to a handy radiator, faucet, or other grounding location. If you're using an anti-static wrist guard, attach it to the same ground as the computer, or connect it to the power supply inside the case, as in **Figure 2.1**. The wristband should fit snug around your wrist and be in constant contact with your skin. Obviously, a long sleeve covering your wrist under the wrist guard won't work.

Loose screws

If your computer's case uses screws, and you open it frequently, you can leave most of the fastening screws off the cover for faster access. Always replace at least one or two fastening screws to prevent accidents.

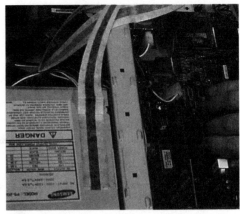

Figure 2.1 The anti-static wrist guard should be grounded to your power supply.

Figure 2.2 Make sure the power is turned off before you open your case.

Is It Sleeping?

Modern PCs have power-saving features that are so convenient you can hardly tell when your computer is off or just sleeping. Be certain it's completely switched off before unplugging it. You can usually tell by looking at the lights on the front of your machine, as in **Figure 2.2**. If the computer is not properly shut down, you may corrupt some files.

PRECAUTIONS AND PREPARATIONS

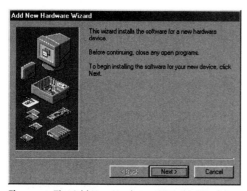

Figure 2.3 The Add New Hardware Wizard in Windows 98 will be a familiar sight after you install a new card.

Windows 3.1 and Plug N Play

Windows 3.1 does not work well with Plug N Play devices. The Windows 3.1 operating environment was introduced long before Plug N Play hardware became available and was never meant to detect or configure these devices. In fact, because Windows 3.1 relies on DOS drivers to use most hardware devices, it does not detect Plug N Play hardware settings. If you are struggling to add and configure new hardware in DOS or Windows 3.1, we recommend that you upgrade your PC to Windows 95 or 98.

Expansion Buses

Configuring new hardware is usually something you think about after you install it, as you see in the Add New Hardware Wizard in **Figure 2.3**. But you can save yourself a great deal of trouble if you consider how you want to configure your computer *before* you perform the surgery. Every new component you put into your system somehow has to talk to your other hardware and software; in fact, many configuration problems are caused by two or more devices trying to talk at the same time, or using the same channels of communication. If this is starting to sound like your in-laws, don't worry. You can solve problems before they happen with a little forethought.

If you are adding an adapter card to your system, note that your motherboard will have specific types of expansion slots and that the adapter card must match an empty slot. Some common types of expansion slots found in PCs today are ISA, VESA, MCA, EISA, and PCI.

✔ Tip

- You should check for available slots before you acquire your new hardware. If all your ISA slots are full, for example, don't buy an ISA internal modem.

EXPANSION BUSES

ISA

Early PCs only had slots that worked with the Industry Standard Architecture bus. A *bus* is a length of cabling or wiring that moves information or electric current. Although most PCs still have a few ISA slots, the ISA bus will probably be phased out of PCs within the next few years because it moves data too slowly for modern components.

✔ Tip

■ ISA slots are usually black—but not always—and may have one or two segments for 8-bit (**Figure 2.4**) and 16-bit (**Figure 2.5**) connectors. An 8-bit ISA adapter card can go in an available 16-bit slot if no 8-bit slots are convenient.

VESA slots in older systems

PC manufacturers switched to a *local bus* to overcome the limitations of the ISA bus. It was called *local* because initially it ran at the same speed as the CPU. The first common type was the VESA bus. VESA was only popular for about two years in the early to mid-1990s, so it's pretty rare to find one today. If your computer has a VESA bus, you definitely should consider upgrading your motherboard or buying a new PC because newer local buses perform better, and adapter cards for VESA systems are almost impossible to find.

VESA slots look like ISA slots (**Figure 2.6**) with an extra segment, usually colored brown. The connectors on the extra VESA segment are smaller and more closely spaced that those on the ISA segments (**Figure 2.7**).

EXPANSION BUSES

Figure 2.4 An ISA 8-bit slot.

Figure 2.5 An ISA 16-bit slot

Figure 2.6 A VESA bus slot, a fairly rare type of local bus today.

Figure 2.7 A VESA bus adapter card.

Figure 2.8 An EISA adapter card.

Figure 2.9 An MCA adapter card.

Figure 2.10 A PCI adapter card.

High-end PCs in the late 1980s used an upgraded ISA bus called the Enhanced Industry Standard Architecture, or EISA (pronounced *ee-sa*) bus (**Figure 2.8**). This bus was mainly used for high-end PC workstations and file servers. It featured an advanced configuration method and a slightly better performance than ISA, but was ultimately replaced by the PCI bus. You won't run into many of these today.

MCA and EISA

You might find a few other types of expansion buses in older PCs. IBM introduced a proprietary bus in the late 1980s called the Micro Channel Architecture, or MCA (**Figure 2.9**). Only IBM-brand PCs used the MCA bus, and because it didn't catch on with the rest of the industry, MCA adapter cards were nearly impossible to buy in stores. Computers that use the MCA bus are likely to be so old that they are no longer in use, but because many people refuse to throw away old computer equipment, you may eventually come across an MCA machine.

PCI

The current state-of-the-art standard for PC expansion slots is the Peripheral Components Interface, or PCI bus. A PCI bus performs better than all previous bus types, and is common in newer PCs, Apple Macintoshes, and a lot of workstation-class hardware like UNIX systems. Strong industry support is likely to keep the PCI bus around for a while.

PCI slots are usually—but not always—white, shorter than ISA slots, and they have connectors that are much thinner than those of the ISA bus, as shown in **Figure 2.10**.

EXPANSION BUSES

Hardware Resources

Each adapter card in the PC requires a unique interrupt (IRQ), input/output address (I/O), and sometimes a direct memory access channel (DMA) to communicate with the CPU.

Interrupts

An interrupt—as the name suggests—is a signal that causes the CPU to stop what it is doing and open communications with the hardware component that sent the interrupt signal. Because the CPU can only communicate with one component at a time, each piece of peripheral hardware must have its own unique interrupt number—and there are only 16 available.

I/O addresses

An I/O address is a location in the computer's memory where the CPU and the hardware component can leave messages for each other.

DMA channels

A DMA channel is a special kind of I/O address that lets a component communicate directly with the system memory without involving the CPU. The arrangement of hardware resources tends to be a source of perpetual confusion and frustration for PC owners because a limited number of these resources are available.

Plug N Play

Happily, you are not expected to configure all the interrupts, addresses, and DMA channels manually. For the last few years PCs have used an automatic configuration procedure called *Plug N Play*. When the computer is booted, it checks all the hardware and assigns unique resource addresses to each component that needs them. The configuration is stored so that it doesn't change unless hardware is added or removed.

Windows 3.1 and the Add New Hardware Wizard

Windows 3.1 does not detect new hardware installed in your PC. Every device that you add must be manually configured—sometimes with a DOS driver, and then again in Windows 3.1 with a Windows 3.1 driver. If you do not perform this configuration, Windows 3.1 will have no clue that a new modem, network card, or video card has been installed. If you replace your video card, for example, Windows 3.1 will try to load the old video adapter drivers to use with your new card. In most cases, this will prevent Windows 3.1 from loading correctly and you will have to run the Windows 3.1 Setup program in DOS to correct the problem. Sound confusing? We agree, and that's why we've upgraded to Windows 95/98.

Plug N Play works in computers that have enough resources for the hardware installed, but it can occasionally cause problems for systems that have a full complement of hardware. If a component requires an interrupt, and one is not available, or if it cannot use a hardware resource in the available ranges, then you will have to manually configure some of your hardware resources. See the section "When Plug N Play fails" later in this chapter.

In order for Plug N Play to work properly, your PC must support it in three ways: Plug N Play adapter cards, Plug N Play motherboard, and a Plug N Play operating system like Windows 95 or 98.

✔ Tip

- When you buy a new PC, make sure that all adapter cards in the system are compatible with Plug N Play, and only purchase Plug N Play cards after that. If even one card is not compatible with the Plug N Play standard, it may cause problems with others.

The motherboard is where the system BIOS (*Basic Input/Output System*) resides (see the section "BIOS" later in this chapter). The BIOS is responsible for booting the computer and loading the operating system. The BIOS must be Plug N Play compatible in order to use Plug N Play hardware. If your computer was built in 1997 or later, chances are its BIOS supports Plug N Play. PCs older than that are good candidates for replacement. If you don't know, look in your computer's manual or check with your computer vendor.

Finally, the operating system must be aware that the BIOS is using Plug N Play to assign hardware resources so that it can read the configuration from the BIOS instead of directly from the hardware.

HARDWARE RESOURCES

Integrated Peripherals

Before you get to work, consider one last hardware issue: the list of integrated peripherals supported by the motherboard.

In the old days, disk drives, printer ports, and serial devices were controlled by adapter cards (**Figure 2.11**). The motherboard did not have any built-in devices to handle these components, so separate cards were needed to run the extra devices. Shortly after the Intel 486 CPU became popular, most of the control electronics that used to reside on these boards moved onto PC motherboards (and the drives themselves) as integrated drive controllers, parallel (printer) ports, and serial (modem, mouse, and printer) ports.

Integrated peripherals reduce the number of expansion slots needed on the motherboard and lower a computer's cost because the total number of adapter cards in each system is reduced. These components still use IRQs, I/O addresses, and DMA channels, and they are still connected to an expansion bus, though not through a slot on the motherboard.

The good news is that now you can control the resource addresses of these integrated peripherals through the BIOS setup menus or Windows 95/98. Before adding any hardware components that use an IRQ, I/O address, or DMA channel, check the settings of all peripheral devices, both integrated ones such as serial ports and non-integrated ones like scanner controllers and sound boards in the Windows Device Manager. It is important to write down the hardware resource configurations of everything in the system before you start to add hardware.

Figure 2.11 The now aged adapter cards that controlled everything from disk drives to printers.

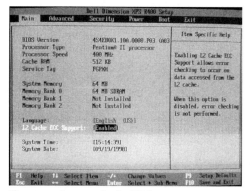

Figure 2.12 An example of a BIOS menu.

BIOS

The BIOS monitors the hardware configuration of the computer, loads the operating system, and allows the operating system to talk to the hardware devices in the machine.

The first thing to know about the BIOS in your PC is how to configure it. A series of setup menus that range from austere, text-based screens to fancy graphical interfaces will give you this information. You commonly access these menus when the computer is booting by pressing specific keys on the keyboard (**Figure 2.12**).

Many motherboards display instructions for entering the BIOS menus when the power is first switched on. However, some motherboard manufacturers are not so forthcoming. If you're not sure how to get into the BIOS of your PC, check the manual that came with it or call the vendor that sold it to you.

The one step at a time rule

Before starting an upgrade, take the time to write down the original value of every setting on every setup screen in the BIOS. Also, if you are changing settings to troubleshoot a problem, change only one setting at a time. You may have to make more than one change to fix a problem, but do them one at a time.

Remember: you must save your configuration and allow the PC to reboot before each set of changes takes effect. Of course, this can take extra time and test your patience, but the information stored in the BIOS is critical to the operation of your computer, and almost every setting has the potential to disable the system.

By experimenting with one setting at a time, you can easily go back to correct any problem introduced. Also, when you solve the problem, you can be reasonably sure that you know which setting change was required.

BIOS

Configuring Adapter Cards

If you are installing and configuring an ISA adapter card, you should review your current hardware resource addresses to make sure that you have at least one free interrupt, and if required, one free DMA channel. Make sure that the adapter card you are installing supports Plug N Play—otherwise you will have to configure it yourself. This manual configuration is a task ideally suited for the expert—or adventurous users wanting to become experts in a hurry.

If you are considering adding an older adapter card that uses jumpers for configuration, you should compare the advantages of simply buying a new Plug N Play card with the frustration and time it will take you to install this old hardware. In this book, we concentrate on the most common hardware available today, which means Plug N Play hardware. If you agree that Plug N Play is the way to go, skip the next section (and avoid hassling with a system that won't work for hours and hours while you mess around inside it). On the other hand, if you are keen to save some money, or to learn more about old PC hardware, read on.

Configuring older adapter cards

In the beginning, PC adapter cards were configured to use a specific interrupt and I/O address with *jumpers*—tiny metal contacts that bridged the gap between two metal posts, as in **Figure 2.13**. One disadvantage to configuring cards with jumpers is that you can't see the configuration settings when the computer case is closed. Checking the current settings or making any changes means turning off the system and opening the case.

Jumpers slide on and off their posts easily. No clips or snaps fasten them; they are held in place by friction alone. Use needlenose pliers to extract or set jumpers that are too hard to

Figure 2.13 A close-up view of jumpers

Figure 2.14 A view of jumper labels on an adapter card.

reach with your fingers. Be sure to check the documentation for the adapter card to determine the correct placement of jumpers. Some adapter cards are marked with a number for each jumper, and in some cases the jumper configurations for each possible IRQ and I/O address are actually printed on the card. This is a real benefit, especially if for some reason the printed documentation for the adapter card is not available (**Figure 2.14**). Although why you'd want to try installing an adapter card with no Plug N Play support and no documentation is beyond us.

Adapter cards that use the EISA bus do not use jumpers to allocate resources. Instead, these cards are configured by running a software utility that programs each card with a unique address. This method proved to be so convenient that eventually ISA cards with programmable IRQ and I/O addresses were released too.

ISA cards that can be programmed with software sometimes also have jumpers for manually overriding software settings. If you wish to configure the cards with software, you'll probably have to remove all the jumpers from the IRQ and I/O settings, or set the jumpers to enable a programmable mode. Note that this is also the case for adapter cards that support Plug N Play and manual jumper settings.

CONFIGURING ADAPTER CARDS

The Add New Hardware Utility

After you install a new adapter card or other piece of hardware, Windows 95/98 should display a message on start up telling you that it has found new hardware. From there you are prompted by a series of dialog boxes to select drivers from Window's own list or to provide a diskette or directory with drivers on it. *Drivers* are programs that allow the operating system to talk to a specific piece of hardware. Drivers are usually very small so that they fit onto a diskette, and new versions can be easily downloaded from the Internet.

If the hardware comes with a driver disk, use it. This is always better than letting Windows provide a generic driver. However, if for some reason you don't have or can't use the vendor's driver, Windows may be able to provide a generic driver. To find out, click the Have Disk button, and start by searching on the Windows CD. If Windows fails to find a driver there, look on your hard disk in the \Windows subdirectory, and if that doesn't work try \Windows\System.

In some cases, Windows may not detect your new hardware. In those cases, you can try to force the operating system to recognize the new hardware by checking *all* the devices in the PC and comparing the current complement with its stored list of components. This is done by running the Add New Hardware Utility. When it detects a device not already on its list, the program knows it has found a new hardware item.

Add New Hardware icon

Figure 2.15 The Add New Hardware icon in the Control Panel.

Figure 2.16 The device list after a new hardware search.

Running the Add New Hardware Utility

1. Click the Start button and open the Settings menu. Click the Control Panel menu item to open the Control Panel.

2. Double click on the Add New Hardware icon in the Control Panel (**Figure 2.15**).

3. Follow the prompts to let Windows detect new hardware.

   At one point you will be allowed the option of skipping auto-detection. Don't do it. Even if you know what you've just added, you should let Windows auto-detect it. Failure to find new devices may be a symptom of an IRQ or I/O address conflict. Or it may reflect a previous installation attempt that failed to complete properly. Sometimes it's impossible to tell why Windows doesn't detect a new piece of hardware.

4. After the detection process is finished, Windows either tells you that it has found new hardware or that no new hardware was found.

   If the component that you added was not detected, then you may try to configure it manually by starting Add New Hardware over and selecting the correct type, brand, and model. However, this is rarely successful. If the new hardware is not correctly detected, you will have to go through a rather drastic and tedious problem-solving procedure. Please see the next section "When the Add New Hardware Wizard won't work."

5. If Windows found new hardware, you can look at the devices it found by clicking on the Details button. It is a good idea to confirm that the device or devices the program found are the actual parts that exist in your PC (**Figure 2.16**).

THE ADD NEW HARDWARE UTILITY

6. Windows will next prompt you to select a driver for the hardware. You should provide the diskette, CD-ROM, or directory where the hardware manufacturer's drivers are located by clicking the Have Disk button (**Figure 2.17**).

7. After the drivers for the new hardware are installed, the computer will almost always reboot itself to load the driver.

After Windows has restarted, your new hardware should be working correctly. If it isn't, don't panic yet! See the rest of this chapter.

When the Add New Hardware Utility won't work

Most of the time, Windows 95/98 does a commendable job finding and configuring new hardware, but it isn't perfect. Occasionally you will install a new component that Windows cannot find or cannot set up. We provide a few tips in the next section to help you solve problems that commonly occur. If you still need more help, your best bet is to contact the manufacturer for further support.

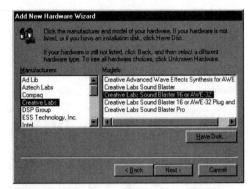

Figure 2.17 The Add New Hardware Wizard's driver selection area.

Other Installation Problems

If you have previously tried to install the component and were not successful, Windows may be retaining information from the previous attempt.

Correcting installation problems

1. Shut down your computer and remove the hardware that you have just installed.

2. Reboot your computer without the new component.

3. After Windows has started and all hard drive activity stops, right-click the My Computer icon and select Properties from the pop-up menu.

4. Click the Device Manager tab in the System Properties dialog window.

5. Look for the device that you were trying to install. You have to know the category in which it is listed, but you can find it if you click through all the categories from top to bottom.

6. If you find the device, select it and click the Remove button to remove it from the configuration.

7. If you do not find the exact device, but a similar device is listed (especially if it appears with an exclamation point icon indicating a conflict) then you should remove it from the Device Manager list.

    Windows may have detected your hardware incorrectly and tried to load the wrong driver, or perhaps something as simple as a disk-read error installing the driver messed up the installation.

    Select this similar device and click the Remove button.

8. If you see any devices listed with a yellow warning icon, you should read the "Correcting interrupt conflicts" section of this chapter before continuing.

   These yellow warning icon devices are either not present in your system or are not properly configured, and they may be interfering with new hardware. If you determine that these devices do not exist in your system, remove them from the Device Manager. By removing them you can force Windows to reconfigure its device list. If they are not present, then they should not come back. If you see more than one or two yellow warning icons, your system needs more configuration help than this book can offer—but try removing them and see if that helps.

9. If you do not find any devices that match your new hardware, and do not see any yellow warning icons, then it is possible that your new hardware is not being correctly configured by the Plug N Play system. See the next section "When Plug N Play won't work."

10. If you removed any devices from the Device Manager, reboot your computer and check the Device Manager again to confirm that the devices have not reappeared. If they do reappear, and you are certain that the hardware is not actually installed, then you can check the following places to delete all references to it.

   Sometimes an installation program will add lines to any of these text files. Open the files with Notepad or another text editing program and look for them with the find utility on the Start menu.

   ◆ CONFIG.SYS

   ◆ AUTOEXEC.BAT

   ◆ WIN.INI

   ◆ SYSTEM.INI

Windows 3.1 and Interrupt Conflicts

Unlike Windows 95/98, Windows 3.1 does not detect and report interrupt conflicts. There is no "Device Manager" in Windows 3.1 that shows you all the hardware devices installed and their hardware settings—you have to track this information yourself. If a hardware device is not functioning correctly you cannot check to see if Windows 3.1 has detected a hardware resource conflict. Instead, you have to guess at the problem until you find the resolution. That's why we refer to Windows 3.1 as the PC GUI Dark Ages.

Make sure you edit carefully! Make a safety copy of each file by copying it with a different name before changing the original. Remove any lines that seem to refer to your new hardware. You will then have to reboot your computer for the change to take effect.

11. Once you are able to reboot your computer and find no unwanted devices listed in the Device Manager, re-install your new hardware and start all over.

Make sure to use the drivers provided by the manufacturer when Windows prompts for them. You may be pleasantly surprised when the installation goes smoothly and successfully. Many times, you will never know why the initial installation failed and the re-installation succeeded. And like most of us, you probably won't care.

As we mentioned, these steps may not resolve all of your installation problems. If you are still having trouble, contact the store where you bought your component or the hardware manufacturer.

When Plug N Play won't work

Plug N Play systems can be a source of as much frustration as earlier, manually configured systems. If you are still using DOS, Windows 3.1, or any other non-Plug N Play-compatible operating system, you may want to consider upgrading to a newer operating system like Windows 95/98—and a new PC if your current system is too elderly to support a new OS.

If you decide to stick with your old clunker and its old operating system, you should disable Plug N Play in the BIOS and set resources manually. DOS must load drivers to communicate with most of the adapter cards in your PC, and those drivers are configured to find each hardware device at a pre-

OTHER INSTALLATION PROBLEMS

determined address (**Figure 2.18**). You will need to select those addresses, interrupts, and DMA channels to access unused resources—by trial and error.

When you add a new hardware device to a Windows 95/98 computer, you should see a message when Windows starts telling you that it has found new hardware. After you install the drivers (and in most cases reboot the computer) you should open the Device Manager to check on the configuration of your new component: right-click the My Computer icon and select Properties from the pop-up menu. Click the Device Manager tab in the System Properties dialog window to see the Device Manager device list.

If you did not see the "Found New Hardware" message when Windows started, or if the device is listed with a yellow warning icon in the Device Manager (or is not listed at all), then you may have an interrupt conflict. We offer a few tips to help you solve some of the common problems that cause interrupt conflicts. If you need more help, you should contact the hardware vendor or retail store where you bought your component.

Correcting interrupt conflicts

1. With the new hardware in the computer, and Windows 95/98 running, open the Device Manager by right-clicking the My Computer icon and selecting Properties from the pop-up menu.

2. Click the Device Manager tab in the System Properties dialog window to see the Device Manager device list.

3. Find the device that you just installed in the list. If you don't know which category it's in, you can click through them all from top to bottom.

4. If there is a yellow warning icon beside the device, then its interrupt number may

Figure 2.18 CONFIG.SYS file loading TSR drivers.

be conflicting with another device in the system. Double-click the device in the list to open the Device Properties dialog box.

Alternatively, your new hardware may have caused another device to stop working. If there is a yellow warning icon beside *another* device, then you should open that device's Device Properties dialog box.

5. Click the Resources tab and check all the items in the Resource Type list box. As you select each item, a message in the conflicting device list will indicate whether there is a problem. Try clicking the Hardware Troubleshooter button for suggestions.

6. You can manually set the value of a conflicting resource by unchecking the Use Automatic Settings checkbox and clicking the Change Settings button. If Windows tells you that you cannot change the settings for the device, then you have to find the device it is conflicting with and change that instead.

7. Use the spin control (up and down buttons) beside the value edit line to scroll through the available resource numbers for this device. A message will appear below to warn you if there are conflicting devices for the new value.

8. After you select a new value and close the Device Properties dialog, you will see a warning telling you that you have overridden the automatic configuration. Click the Yes button to continue.

9. When you close the System Properties dialog box, you will be prompted to reboot your computer. After it restarts, you should open the Device Manager again to confirm that there are no more interrupt conflicts.

OTHER INSTALLATION PROBLEMS

If you are unable to resolve your problem with the preceding steps, there are a few more changes you can try. Some hardware devices cannot use certain interrupts, even if they are free. If you force a device to use a different interrupt in order to free up one that is suitable for your new hardware, you may fix your problem. Also, if you are running out of interrupts, you can try to disable a serial port or the printer port if you don't need it. This is done in the system BIOS—see the section "BIOS" earlier in this chapter, which describes how to make changes there.

✔ Tips

- A patient, painstaking, step-by-step approach will often succeed in resolving resource conflicts. Make a list of current resource assignments before you start, and methodically change them, one by one, until all your hardware works.

- Be sure to keep written notes of what you are doing so you can reverse anything that causes trouble.

- Remember, you may need to change the interrupt assignments in driver software (such as a sound driver) to match a change in the hardware interrupt of your sound board, and then reboot the system before you see any improvement. This is why computer techies get paid a lot of money. See the last chapter of this book for more information about interrupts before attempting to change them.

- In some cases you may install hardware that does not show up in the Device Manager at all. This is not always a symptom of a problem. Some devices require that the manufacturer's drivers be installed before the hardware works at all. You should *always* refer to the documentation that came with your hardware before installing it.

Don't Fear Your Hardware

It is true that a few procedures in this book can potentially cause permanent damage to your computer hardware, but in those cases we explicitly warn you when any step of any hardware upgrade carries this risk. So don't be afraid to make changes to the hardware settings in your computer when you're upgrading or trying to solve problems.

Of course, you may become hopelessly confused when first experimenting with all the possible resource configurations in a PC, and we don't advise making unnecessary changes to a system you depend on. However, by starting with small projects, being persistent, and using the information in this book, you'll eventually gain the confidence to perform any upgrade or hardware reconfiguration that you are ever likely to encounter. Ultimately, you'll be able to use what you learn to build your own PC from components. Most people find that putting a computer together is a lot easier than they imagined!

Upgrading the BIOS

Most modern motherboards feature the ability to upgrade the BIOS via flash-ROM chips programmed by utilities that you can download on the manufacturer's Web site. This simple upgrade can improve the performance and compatibility of your Plug N Play system and improve other features of your computer. You should be aware that there is a risk involved, so upgrading for no reason is not always prudent.

Upgrading the BIOS usually involves downloading a program from a Web site. Copy it to a floppy disk. Then boot the computer from the floppy and either follow the onscreen instructions or allow the process to proceed automatically. For more information and complete instructions, visit the Web site of your computer or motherboard manufacturer.

UPGRADING THE BIOS

MODEMS AND NETWORK DEVICES

Most users connect to the Internet with a modem—either an internal model (a modem card) or an external model (a small box that sits beside your computer. Your computer can also communicate with other machines via a network, which amounts to a set of adapter cards and cables linking two or more machines together. Networks are becoming increasingly common even in the home, for everything from sharing printers and modems to multi-player gaming.

This chapter covers the installation and configuration of the hardware your computer uses to communicate with other computers. We show you how to get network cards, modem cards, and external modems up and running on your computer.

Network Interface Cards

The most important considerations for choosing a network card are cost, speed, and compatibility. If you are connecting to an existing *local area network* (LAN), then some of these factors are already decided for you—you simply have to buy a *network interface card* (NIC) that is compatible with your LAN.

On the other hand, setting up a LAN from scratch leaves all kinds of complicated decisions up to you. That's really a bit beyond the scope of a simple upgrade, but if you are determined to undertake this huge task, take the time to learn more about computer networking before you begin. We'll offer some basics to get you started.

Why set up a LAN? A computer network allows you to share and copy files between two or more computers. It also allows you to share devices like modems, printers, and Internet connections.

A computer network can be server-based, peer-to-peer, or a combination of the two:

A **server-based LAN** includes at least one computer whose only function is to act as the "server"—to provide files, printing, and other services to the other "workstation" computers. The workstations cannot connect to each other directly; they can only communicate with each other through the server.

A **peer-to-peer network** lets every computer on the LAN connect to every other computer directly. We focus on peer-to-peer, as they provide all the features that most home and small office users need. Server-based LANs usually require you to buy special (expensive) software; Windows 95/98 comes out of the box with all the software you need to set up a peer-to-peer LAN.

✔ Tip

■ If you are connecting to a server-based network, or some kind of hybrid, be sure to consult with the network administrator before you begin.

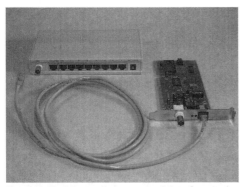

Figure 3.1 An Ethernet hub, a network interface card (NIC), and a cable. The hub connects all the cables in a network.

LAN Hardware

Networking hardware varies somewhat, but commonly requires a network interface card and a network cable for each computer. Some networks require a *hub* (the box shown at the top left of **Figure 3.1**) to connect all the network cables together; others simply run a cable from one computer to the next in a *daisy chain*.

Common network hardware ideal for small offices or homes is reasonably priced and provides 10 megabits per second (mbps) performance. This speed is the best for a home network, and is more than adequate for networked computer games.

Hardware for a simple LAN

For small office or home users setting up a network for the first time, we recommend you use the following:

◆ **A 10 base T or 100 base T Ethernet network hub.** The hub is the central box to which each computer connects. The "10" or "100" indicates how fast the network can communicate. The hub must have enough ports to accommodate all computers, printers, and other devices that you want to connect. It is probably the single most expensive piece of hardware you'll need to purchase for your network. In most cases an eight-port hub is normally enough for a small computer network. (If you're connecting to an existing network, and it uses a hub-based topology, the hub is already there.)

◆ **A 10 base T or 100 base T Ethernet network interface card (NIC).** This is an adapter card that connects to the cable that ties your machine to the other computers on the LAN. You'll pay a little more for a 100 base T card, but it's worth it for the higher speed. Even if you're currently running on a 10 mbps network, a 100 base T card will work fine, and when you upgrade your hub the new card will support the higher speed. You need an NIC for each computer on your network. One word of warning: strictly speaking, it is not necessary to install identical NICs for all the computers on your network, but it is generally a very good idea.

◆ **A category 5 (Cat 5) unshielded twisted pair (UTP) network cable with RJ-45 connectors at both ends.** (If you thought you'd heard a lot of computer jargon before, just wait until you set up a computer network!) This is a common type of network cable, very easy to find in most computer stores. You will need a network cable for each computer on your network.

✔ Tip

■ If you have the budget, sure, a 100 base T hub is a great upgrade, but you probably won't need the extra performance for quite a while. Even the fastest Internet connection commonly available to home and small office users is nowhere near the capacity of a 10 mbps network, and current multi-player games don't need the extra speed, either. The only advantage that a 100 mbps network will afford is faster file transfers between computers.

What Is Ethernet?

Computers communicate on a LAN by sending little messages called *packets* along the network cable. Depending on the network topology, these packets may pass though some or all of the other computers on their way to the intended recipient. In an Ethernet network, every packet goes to every other computer at close to the same time, as if it were travelling through the "ether"—the mystical medium through which all electromagnetic energy was once thought to flow.

In other topologies, such as *token-ring* networks, a computer sends a packet to the next computer along the ring. If the packet is not meant for that computer, it passes the "token" to the next machine until it reaches the correct destination.

There are costs and benefits to Ethernet. Since each packet reaches every computer at about the same time, the network performance is very good—as long as only one computer is trying to send a packet. As more machines are added to the network, more packets are sent at once and they collide, canceling themselves out. These messages must then be re-sent, which degrades network throughput.

Token ring networks give each computer its own turn to send messages, so packets do not collide. However, each computer must wait for its turn to send a message. This means that on a small network, Ethernet will be faster than token ring, but on a large, busy network, token ring may offer faster performance. Be that as it may, token ring is a relatively rare topology. Almost all networks, big and small, use Ethernet hardware.

Figure 3.2 The Windows 95/98 CD-ROMs contain networking software and are easy to use and configure.

LAN Software

Windows 95/98 supports almost all the hardware currently used for networking computers.

While you *can* use other network operating systems (NOSs), such as Netware, for your LAN, Windows 95 and 98 are the simplest to configure and use. Best of all, Windows 98 comes with almost every new PC (**Figure 3.2**). For that reason, we will deal mainly with Windows when we're talking about networking software.

Windows 3.1 and Peer to Peer Networking

Windows 3.1 computers can share resources with each other on a LAN just like Windows 95/98 computers, but you need a special version called Windows for Workgroups 3.11. This version provides file and printer sharing with other Microsoft Windows Networking clients like Windows NT, Windows 95/98, and Windows 3.11. It does not, however, make installing a network interface card any easier than installing other types of new hardware in Windows 3.1.

Installing a Network Interface Card

No matter which type of LAN you use, installing an NIC in your PC is usually required. First, we show you what to do before you even crack open the computer case, and then we tell you how to insert the NIC.

NIC pre-installation

Before you buy an NIC for your computer(s), check for available bus slots in each PC. New network cards use PCI slots, but you may be able to find older cards that use the ISA bus.

Most new NICs available today use the Plug N Play standard to configure hardware resources in your PC. You should always look for this type of hardware when buying new components.

NIC installation

1. Make certain that your PC is turned off and unplugged, and then open the case.

2. Locate an empty bus slot that matches the type of NIC adapter card you are adding.

3. Remove the expansion port cover from the back of the computer case that corresponds to the bus slot you're using (**Figure 3.3**).

   Be sure to carefully set aside the screw that holds the port cover down.

4. Slide the NIC into the bus slot so that the metal flange on the card fits into the expansion port, and the metal contacts on the edge of the card fit into the slot (**Figure 3.4**).

5. Make sure the card is pushed all the way into the slot. Although some cases prevent adapter cards from fitting all the way into the bus slot, the card must at least fit well enough to make contact with all the metal connectors in the slot.

Figure 3.3 Remove the slot cover.

Figure 3.4 Push the card into the slot.

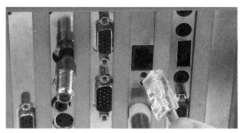

Figure 3.5 Attach the network cable.

6. Use the screw you removed from the port cover to fasten the NIC to the case.

7. Attach the network cable to the port on the back of the NIC, as in **Figure 3.5**.

✔ Tip

■ At this point you will be tempted to put the case back on and screw it closed. Don't do it. After you complete *all* software configuration and testing you can re-attach the cover, but it is much more convenient to leave it off now, in case you have to remove and replace the card several times. If you put the case back together before you've configured the software, you'll learn quickly that it pays to wait until everything is running properly to reassemble your machine.

Two Cards in One Machine?

It is possible to install two network cards in a Windows 95/98 machine. The Plug N Play system should configure each card with a unique interrupt and I/O address, as long as there are enough free hardware resources. After you complete the installation you should confirm both network cards' settings in the Windows Device Manager.

Why would you ever need two network cards in one computer? In some areas there are high-speed Internet connections available using cable modems, ISDN, or ADSL technologies. These connections communicate with your computer through a standard Ethernet network adapter card. If you already have a LAN set up and you want to have a computer connected to the fast Internet connection and your own network at the same time, it will require two NICs. As a benefit, if you install proxy or gateway software on this computer, all the other PCs on your network can access the Internet through its high-speed connection. For more information, search the Web for "Proxy Servers."

NIC software configuration

1. With the newly installed NIC in the computer, and the case cover still off, turn on your PC.

2. If you have installed an NIC that requires you to use a special configuration program to set resources, use it now (**Figures 3.6** and **3.7**).

3. When Windows 95/98 starts, you'll see a message telling you that Windows has found new hardware, as in **Figure 3.8**.

   If you do not see this message, don't panic! Well, okay, panic a little and then turn back to the section "The Add New Hardware Utility" in Chapter 2.

   After Windows finds the new hardware, it will prompt you for drivers that enable the operating system to use the new card, as in **Figure 3.9**.

Figure 3.6 The NIC configuration menu.

Figure 3.7 The configuration utility may give you an error message.

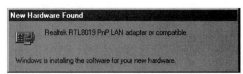

Figure 3.8 The New Hardware Found dialog box tells you that Windows recognizes the new hardware.

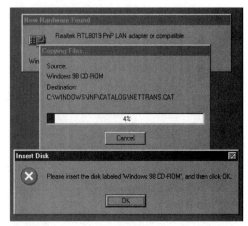

Figure 3.9 The New Hardware Drivers dialog box is Windows's prompt for the drivers.

Figure 3.10 You will likely use an NIC configuration utility diskette or a CD-ROM.

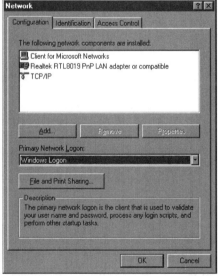

Figure 3.11 The Network dialog box shows which network protocols are installed on your PC.

If your NIC came with a diskette or CD-ROM with drivers (**Figure 3.10**), you should insert it now and point Windows to the correct drive. If for some reason you do not have the manufacturer's drivers for your NIC, or it is not working properly, you can let Windows try to find a driver from its own library. Click the "Have Disk" button, and start by searching on your Windows CD. If Windows fails to find a driver there, look on your hard disk in the \Windows subdirectory, and if that doesn't work try \Windows\System.

4. After Windows installs the driver and reboots, configure the network protocols that you want Windows to use (**Figure 3.11**). Please see the next section for more information about network protocols. The default settings should enable you to see other Windows computers on the network.

Setting Up Your LAN

Once you've installed your NIC, the battle is only half over. Now you have to configure your network protocols properly so that your computer recognizes, and can be recognized by, other computers on the LAN. Follow these steps to get you on the right network track.

Configuring network protocols for workstations on a LAN

1. Decide which network protocol or protocols you want to use on your LAN (see the nearby sidebar "Selecting a Network Protocol").

   If you are connecting to an existing LAN, then these decisions have already been made, so consult with the network administrator and just do what everybody else is doing.

2. Open the Windows Control Panel and double-click the Network icon. Alternatively, right-click the Network Neighborhood icon on your desktop and select Properties from the pop-up menu.

3. In the Network dialog window find the list box labeled, "The following network components are installed" (**Figure 3.12**). Ideally, this list box will show at least these four items:

   ◆ Client for Microsoft Networks.

   ◆ LAN adapter (the name of the adapter depends on the NIC installed in your system).

   ◆ At least one protocol.

   ◆ File and printer sharing for Microsoft networks.

   Keep reading to find out how to change the existing list. Note that if you have a modem installed that you use to connect

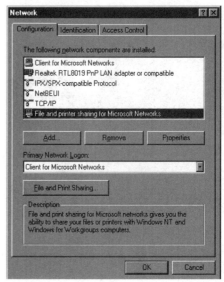

Figure 3.12 The Network Properties dialog box lists network components that are installed.

Windows 3.1 and Network Card Software

Windows for Workgroups 3.11 comes with a library of drivers for many network interface cards. Unfortunately, it has been many years since Windows for Workgroups 3.11 was released, and this list does not include most recent network cards. Worse yet, most recent network cards do not include Windows 3.1 or Windows for Workgroups 3.11 drivers. Without the proper drivers, you cannot use the networking hardware inside your computer.

If you do manage to find network interface cards that work under Windows 3.1, you can configure all network settings with the Network icon in the Control Panel.

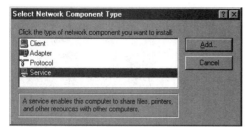

Figure 3.13 The Select Network Component Type dialog box allows you to select the networking item you want to add.

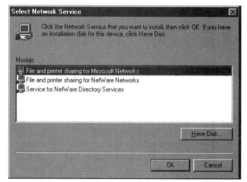

Figure 3.14 Click the "Have Disk" button to locate your network software.

to the Internet, it will probably be listed here along with the TCP/IP protocol.

✔ Tips

- By default, most Windows machines will install an item called "Client for Netware Networks." Unless you are connecting to a LAN that includes a Netware server, you can delete this item.

- If you want to see shared resources on other computers on your LAN, you will have to add the item called "File and printer sharing for Microsoft networks." Instructions for adding items are in the following steps in this list.

- To add a protocol or other item to the Network component list box, click the Add button.

- In the Select Network Component Type dialog box, click the type of networking item you want to add, as in **Figure 3.13**.
  Protocols include TCP/IP, IPX, and NetBEUI.
  Services include "File and printer sharing."
  Clients include support for Netware networks and Microsoft networking.
  When you have highlighted a component type, click the Add button.

- When adding a client, select a manufacturer and client from the list displayed. Note, though, that it is rare to add a new network client program to your Windows machine because the client for Microsoft networks is installed by default, and other clients are not usually required.

- When adding a service, select the service you want from the list that appears in **Figure 3.14**. If you have a diskette or directory with new networking service software, click the Have Disk button and follow the prompts to locate the software.

■ When adding a protocol, Windows will build a driver information database and then present a list of available manufacturers and network protocols. Unless you are attaching your computer to an existing LAN with computers configured to use another manufacturer's network operating system, you should always choose Microsoft as the manufacturer.

■ When adding a protocol, after clicking on Microsoft in the manufacturer list, you will see a list of available protocols. Depending on which version of Windows 95 or 98 you are using, this list may be quite long or quite short. For most people setting up a LAN, the only important protocols to consider are NetBEUI, IPX, or TCP/IP. Select the protocol you want (see the section "Selecting a network protocol" later in this chapter) and click OK, as in **Figure 3.15**.

The TCP/IP protocol requires you to configure some settings before it can be used. See the section "Configuring the TCP/IP Protocol" later in this chapter.

■ Windows will copy the selected software to your system and take you back to the Network dialog window where you started. You must add each protocol separately, so if you want to add more protocols follow steps 4 to 9 for each one you add.

■ When the components list box displays all the networking components you need, click the OK button on the Network dialog window.

Windows will think for a moment and then tell you that it wants to restart. Each time you make a change to network settings, Windows has to restart, so if you have multiple items to configure, make sure you change them all at once and then let your computer restart.

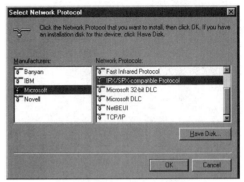

Figure 3.15 Select the network protocol you want.

Windows 3.1 and Setting Up Your LAN

In the heyday of Windows 3.1, the most common way of networking a Windows PC was to load DOS drivers for the network interface card and then load Windows 3.1 without any special network configuration. Because DOS provided the networking, Windows 3.1 simply thought it was using DOS disk drives and printers. The most common networking software in those days was Novell Netware, which was a server-based LAN architecture. If you can find this software today, you can still use it to network Windows 3.1 PCs. But it is much simpler to switch to Windows 95/98.

Selecting a network protocol

You must install at least one network protocol or your computer won't be able to communicate on the network. Each machine on the network must use the same protocol. You can use more than one if you want, but it is a good idea to install just the protocols that you need.

Selecting one or more networking protocols can be confusing. A PC LAN can use three of the most popular protocols: TCP/IP (also called IP), IPX, and NetBEUI.

TCP/IP. We recommend that you use TCP/IP as the only protocol on your network. There are many reasons this is a good idea: Since it is the protocol used on the Internet, you will need to have TCP/IP installed if you connect your LAN to the Internet later on. Also, most PC games now use TCP/IP for multi-player sessions. If you run a Web-server as part of an office Intranet, then you will have to use TCP/IP to connect to it with a Web browser from other computers on your network. TCP/IP also supports Windows file and printer sharing, so you will have full access to shared resources on your LAN. Finally, if you ever decide to add non-PC devices to your computer network, they will most likely use the TCP/IP protocol.

There are drawbacks to the TCP/IP protocol, though. Compared to NetBEUI and IPX, it is relatively difficult to configure, because you have to provide a network address and other information for each computer on the LAN. The other protocols provide this information automatically, without any work on your part. Also, if you do connect your LAN to the Internet through a gateway or proxy server at some point, you will have to be aware of some security issues. If you plan to do this, invest in a good Internet security book or other reference.

IPX. If you play computer games—especially older DOS games—you'll probably need to use the IPX protocol. Novell introduced the IPX/SPX protocol in its Netware network operating system. Most games published when Netware was by far the most popular LAN software used IPX to communicate. Even today, some Windows 95/98 games use IPX when they're played on a LAN.

NetBEUI. Simple networks in which a few workstations need file and printer sharing can use the NetBEUI protocol. NetBEUI is the easiest protocol to install and configure, since it pretty much just works once you install it. If you don't plan to do anything except share printers and files on your network then you should choose this protocol.

Fortunately, Windows 95 and 98 supports all three protocols. You can even use all three protocols at the same time, though it is a good idea to use only those you need. Since Windows can use TCP/IP or IPX for file and printer sharing, you rarely need to install NetBEUI except on simple networks where you won't be installing TCP/IP or IPX. Some network cards and their software drivers do not handle multiple protocols very elegantly, so if you come across unexplained networking problems, try removing unneeded networking protocols one at a time to isolate the problem.

Setting Up Your LAN

Configuring the TCP/IP Protocol

The TCP/IP protocol is a versatile communication language for networked computers, which is one reason it is used on the Internet. Unfortunately, this versatility means that it requires some configuring before it works properly.

All computers using TCP/IP must be given a unique network address, and that address must be set in software. You will also have to set the range of other addresses that a computer can see, as well as the way the computer will try to find an address that it cannot directly see. We don't have room to fully treat TCP/IP networking in this book. The following procedure is offered only as a bare-bones, simple way to configure your TCP/IP network. Ideally, if you are interested in setting up and configuring a TCP/IP network, you should consult a networking book or other reference that can fully explain it.

Configuring TCP/IP settings in Windows 95 and 98

1. Open the Windows Control Panel and double-click on the Network icon.

2. In the Network window, double-click the TCP/IP protocol listed in the network components list box.

   This will open the TCP/IP Properties window. If you have an NIC and a modem installed in your PC, you will see the TCP/IP protocol listed twice. Pick the one that points to the network adapter and leave the one for the dial-up adapter unchanged.

3. Click on the IP Address tab at the top of the TCP/IP Properties window, click the "Specify an IP address" radio button, and type an address into the IP Address edit box.

Give your first computer an address of **192.168.0.1** and increment the fourth octet (the "1") for each subsequent computer to insure that each computer has a unique address. For instance, the next computer in the LAN would be addressed as **192.168.0.2**.

4. In the Subnet Mask edit box (**Figure 3.16**) type **255.255.255.0**. See the nearby sidebar "The Truth About IP" for more on the meaning of these numbers.

5. Click the WINS Configuration tab and make sure that WINS is disabled (**Figure 3.17**).

6. Click the Gateway tab (**Figure 3.18**). For small networks that are not connected to any other network, you don't need to specify a gateway. And more complicated networks are beyond the scope of this chapter.

7. Click the DNS Configuration tab (**Figure 3.19**). Like the gateway, it is not necessary to configure a domain name server (DNS) for isolated LANs, so make sure DNS is *disabled*. Multi-segmented networks and wide-area links are beyond the scope of this chapter.

8. The default settings for the other tabs in the TCP/IP Properties dialog window are fine for most small LANs, so click the OK button to finish the configuration.

   After your protocols are configured and you have rebooted you should be able to see other nodes on your network (look in Network Neighborhood or Windows Explorer).

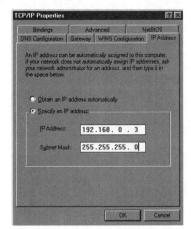

Figure 3.16 Entering the subnet mask.

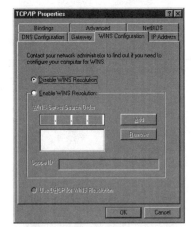

Figure 3.17 Make sure WINS is disabled.

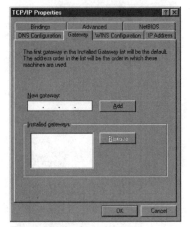

Figure 3.18 Checking the Gateway.

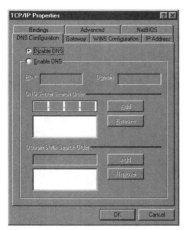

Figure 3.19 Click the DNS Configuration tab.

Figure 3.20 Pick "sharing" from the pop-up menu in this dialog box.

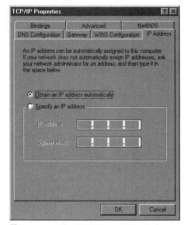

Figure 3.21 The TCP Properties dialog box allows you to enter IP addresses.

To see files on other computers, you must install the file and printer sharing service on the host machine and then share out directories or printers (**Figure 3.20**). Do this in Windows Explorer by right-clicking on a directory or printer and selecting Sharing from the pop-up menu. The Sharing dialog is very straightforward: click the "shared as" radio button and click OK.

The Truth About IP

An IP address is composed of four *octets* of information, or four numbers each between 0 and 255, separated by dots. If you are configuring a small LAN to use the IP protocol, you can use a range of IP addresses reserved for private networks. These address do not exist anywhere on the Internet, which makes them a suitable choice for private networks. (Even if you do connect your network to the Internet, you won't have to worry about address conflicts with other computers already connected.)

The IP address range of 192.168.0.1 to 192.168.255.255 is the private range you can use for your LAN. Unless you have more than 255 nodes on your network you should set all addresses to use the same number in the third octet (we suggest 0, but you can pick anything between 0 and 255). Each computer must have a unique number in the fourth octet. If you have more than 255 devices on your LAN, then you probably have access to better resources than we can provide here. Some ISPs require that you obtain an IP address automatically (**Figure 3.21**) .

CONFIGURING THE TCP/IP PROTOCOL

Modems

Like network cards (NICs), modems usually come down to cost versus performance. Older modems that are only capable of slow connection speeds like 28.8 kilobits per second are quite cheap. The newest modems that support the highest available speeds—currently 56 kilobits per second (kbps)—are priced somewhat higher. Most users find that a faster modem makes Web surfing and even email communications much more fun, and is worth the additional cost.

Figure 3.22 Modems can be either internal (right) or external (left).

You can buy a modem in two flavors: internal and external. Internal modems come in the form of an internal adapter card that fits into your computer; external modems are small boxes that sit somewhere outside your computer's case and connect by cable to the back of your computer. There's no significant difference in performance speed, so the only issue is deciding whether you prefer an internal or external setup.

✔ Tip

- External modems are more expensive, but offer one huge advantage. If your Internet connection hangs up, sometimes the only way to reset it and resume telecommunications is to turn off the modem and turn it back on. If it's external, this can be done with two flips of a switch. If it's internal, the only way to turn it off and on is to reset the entire PC.

The next two sections walk you through installing both internal and external modems. See **Figure 3.22** for examples of both.

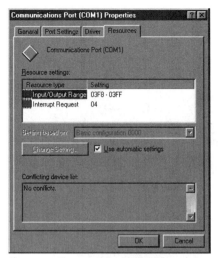

Figure 3.23 Set your IRQ and I/O addresses in the Modem COM port resources box.

Figure 3.24 If your modem has jumpers, shown here on a modem card, set them to the correct locations.

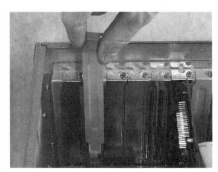

Figure 3.25 Remove the port/slot cover.

Internal modem pre-installation

1. Go into your system's BIOS setup menu. To get to it, you usually hold down a key while the computer is in the first few seconds of booting. If there is no message displayed like "Press DEL to enter setup" when you turn on your computer then you should consult your system or motherboard documentation, or contact the vendor.

2. Find the BIOS setup menu that allows you to disable COM1 or COM2. If you have a mouse that plugs into a serial port (the connector usually has nine pins and looks a little like a "D"), then you must not disable the serial COM port that your mouse uses. If you have a PS/2 style mouse (the connector is round) then you may disable COM1 or COM2.

3. All new internal modems use Plug N Play to set the IRQ and I/O address in Windows 95/98 (**Figure 3.23**). It is rare to find a modem that still uses jumpers (**Figure 3.24**), and well-worth the price of a new Plug N Play unit to avoid the frustration of setting interrupts and I/O addresses.

Internal modem installation

1. Make certain that your PC is turned off and unplugged, then open the case.

2. Locate an empty bus slot that matches the type of modem adapter card you are adding.

3. Remove the expansion port cover from the back of the computer case that corresponds to the bus slot you're using (**Figure 3.25**). Put the screw that held the port cover down in a safe place.

(continued)

MODEMS

4. Slide the modem into the bus slot so that the metal flange on the card fits into the expansion port. Also ensure that the metal contacts on the edge of the card fit into the slot.

5. Check to see that the card is pushed all the way into the bus slot.

   Some cases prevent adapter cards from sitting all the way into the bus slot, but the card must fit well enough to make contact with all the metal contacts in the slot, as in **Figure 3.26**.

Figure 3.26 Push the card all the way into the slot.

6. Fasten the modem to the case with the screw you removed from the port cover.

7. Attach the telephone line cable to the phone line port on the back of the modem (**Figure 3.27**).

✔ Tips

- Because most modems have two phone jacks to allow for a phone, be sure to plug the line from the phone jack on the wall into the correct jack on the modem. It is usually labeled "Line."

Figure 3.27 Plug in the telephone jack to the back of the modem.

- Leave the computer case cover off. After you've finished the software configuration and testing, you can replace the cover, but until then, you'll find it's more convenient to leave it off.

Windows 3.1 and Modem Speed

One major disadvantage of using Windows 3.1 with a modem is that it only supports modem speeds up to 19.2 kbps. That means you cannot get the full use of your 28.8, 33.6, or 56 kpbs modem if you are running Windows 3.1.

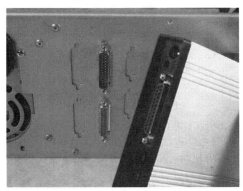

Figure 3.28 You must connect a COM (serial) port with your eternal modem.

Figure 3.29 A serial cable connects the two ports.

External modem installation

1. Check the back of your computer for a free serial port connector.

   The serial port connector can be either a wide 15-pin or narrow 9-pin "D" connector (one side is wider than the other, which forms a rough "D" shape). The pins are arranged into two rows. Both are shown in **Figure 3.28**.

2. Use a serial cable to connect the modem to the COM port on the back of the PC (see **Figure 3.29**).

   You may need a port adapter that converts the 9-pin connector on the serial cable to the 15-pin connector on the case, or vice versa; neither effects the performance of an external modem.

3. Connect the phone line to the correct jack on the back of the modem.

4. Connect the power supply to the external modem and make sure the modem is switched on *before* rebooting your PC. If the power is left off, Windows will not detect the new hardware when it starts.

Windows 3.1 and Modems

Windows 3.1 provided only the most basic support for modems. It allowed Windows 3.1 applications to use the modem without having to be individually configured. Since the Internet was not yet popular, Windows 3.1 did not provide an easy way to dial into an Internet Service Provider and connect to the Internet—you had to install separate software just to do that. Windows 95/98 makes the dial-up procedure very simple.

MODEMS

Modem Software

Now that you've got that modem all hooked up and ready to go, you've got to tackle the last remaining obstacle: installing the software. This section shows you how to get over this last hurdle and begin surfing the Net with your new modem.

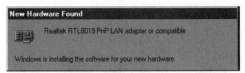

Figure 3.30 Once Windows senses your new card, it'll show you the Found New Hardware message.

Configuring your modem driver

1. With the newly installed modem card in the computer and the case cover still left off (or the newly attached external modem powered on), turn on your PC.

   If you detached any of the connections while installing the modem, re-attach them before turning on the computer.

2. After your computer starts, you should see a message telling you that Windows has found new hardware (**Figure 3.30**).

   If you do not see this message, don't panic. Instead, read the section in Chapter 2 called "The Add New Hardware Utility."

3. After Windows finds the new hardware, it will prompt you for drivers to enable the operating system to use the modem. Insert the diskette or CD-ROM that came with the modem and point to the correct drive letter so that Windows can load the manufacturer's drivers.

   If you do not have drivers provided by the manufacturer, you may be able to let Windows detect and load drivers from its library. Make sure you have the Windows setup CD-ROM handy. Click the "Have Disk" button, and start by searching on the Windows CD. If Windows fails to find a driver there, look on your hard disk in the \Windows subdirectory, and if that doesn't work try \Windows\System.

4. After Windows installs the driver and reboots, you are ready to use your new

No COM Port?

Most newer computers have two COM ports on the back side. If both of your ports are in use, or if your PC is so old it only has one, you may be able to add an inexpensive adapter card to your computer that will provide additional serial devices.

Also, you should be aware that if you bought a generic "bargain-brand" PC there may be connectors on the back of you computer than don't actually connect to anything inside the case. This may also be true if your computer has been frequently upgraded or modified. If you have a problem with an external modem, open the case and confirm that the port into which it is plugged is actually connected to something inside the case.

MODEM SOFTWARE

Figure 3.31 The Add/Remove Programs Properties dialog box—make sure all Communications components are installed.

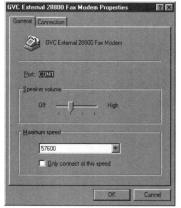

Figure 3.32 Our modem's Properties dialog box.

modem. If you plan to use the modem to connect to another computer to share files or to connect to the Internet, make sure you have installed all the Communications components including "Dial-up Networking" in the Windows Setup tab of the Add/Remove Programs Properties dialog box (**Figure 3.31**).

5. Windows 95/98 does most of the proper configuring of new modems automatically. To check the settings that Windows has used, open the Control Panel and double-click the Modems icon to open the modem's Properties dialog box (**Figure 3.32**). The most important setting to check is the serial port line speed (see the nearby sidebar "Checking the Modem Serial Port Line Speed."

Modem sounds

In the modem configuration dialog box, you can set the modem volume to mute all sounds the device makes. If the hissing and buzzing of the modem annoys you whenever you make a call, you can turn off the speaker.

Generally, though, it's a good idea to leave the volume on so that you're aware of any problems that come up, such as a person answering the phone instead of a modem, or the phone line not being answered at all.

But if you call the same phone number routinely and are certain that the connection will be successful, go ahead and turn off the volume if you want.

Checking the Modem Serial Port Line Speed

Testing a modem is a pretty simple process. In the Control Panel, double-click the Modems icon and select the Diagnostics tab in the Modems Properties dialog box. Click the Diagnostics (or More Info) button to let Windows attempt to communicate with the modem. If it is working, you will see a list of diagnostic responses from the modem.

DISK

DEVICES

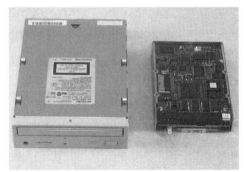

Figure 4.1 Upgrading your hard drive or CD-ROM drive isn't as difficult as you might think. Here are a couple of typical drives.

Perhaps the most common problem today's computer users have is running out of hard drive space. As Internet access (with its flood of downloaded files storing themselves on the disk) becomes more commonplace, and software becomes extra bloated, hard drive space is at a premium on most home PCs.

Good, fast CD-ROM and DVD-ROM (**Figure 4.1**) drives are increasingly desirable and affordable. In fact, most software now ships on CD-ROM anyway. So, if your CD-ROM drive is slow, broken, or missing altogether, upgrading it can be considered critical to keeping your system current.

Adding or replacing the hard drive, CD-ROM, or DVD drive in a PC is one of the easier upgrades you can tackle, but even so you may encounter a few pitfalls. This chapter will guide you through the process toward a fast, painless upgrade.

There are two types of disk devices used in personal computers today. Most PCs use EIDE (Enhanced Integrated Drive Electronics) hard disks and CD-ROM drives. EIDE hardware is cheap and performs well enough for most users. High-performance PCs use SCSI (Small Computer System Interface—pronounced "scuzzy") drives. SCSI hardware is more expensive than EIDE but performs better, and the modern SCSI bus can handle up to 15 devices. We will be covering the following hard drive upgrade procedures in this chapter.

1. Adding an EIDE hard disk as a second disk drive. This is the easiest way to add drive capacity to your system.

2. Adding a SCSI hard disk as a second disk drive. Most SCSI bus adapters can support up to 15 devices, so systems with these types of drives are easier to upgrade with additional devices.

3. Replacing the primary disk drive in your computer. This is more complicated than simply adding a new disk drive, but it is necessary if you want to change the disk drive from which your system boots.

DISK DEVICES

Figure 4.2 An old IDE drive controller adapter card. If you have one of these, it is time for an upgrade.

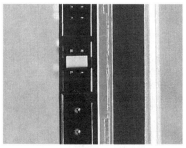

Figure 4.3 Set the jumpers to master or slave by using the jumpers on the back of the drive.

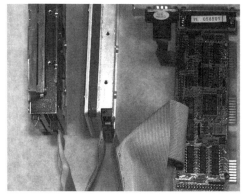

Figure 4.4 You can put two EIDE drives on one EIDE drive connector.

Installing an EIDE Drive

EIDE hard drives are the most common type of drive in PCs today. The EIDE standard is a follow-up to the IDE standard that was used for many years. In the unlikely event that you are upgrading a computer that still has IDE disk drives in it, you should be aware that new EIDE drives will not work with the IDE connector in your system. You may be able to find an EIDE adapter card to add to your system, but it is probably better to buy a new PC since IDE systems are way past their useful lifetimes.

How do you know if your disk connector is for IDE or EIDE drives? If your PC has a 486 or older CPU, chances are good that it is IDE. If your CPU is a Pentium, most likely you have EIDE connectors. If you want to know for sure, check your system manual or call the manufacturer.

Figure 4.2 shows an example of an IDE drive controller adapter card. Note that the connector is exactly the same size as the new EIDE connector—but don't be fooled: You cannot run an EIDE drive with this IDE controller.

Preparing to install an EIDE hard drive

1. Set the drive to be the master or slave device using the jumpers on the back of the drive, as in **Figure 4.3**, or with DIP switches, which some manufacturers use. For specific instructions, check the documentation that came with the drive. Also, see the next section "Master/slave settings for EIDE drives."

2. If you're installing a second hard drive on your system, you need to check the master/slave settings for the drive already in your computer. **Figure 4.4** shows the connection of two drives to a drive connector.

3. If you are installing a hard disk and a CD-ROM on the same EIDE connector, their master/slave settings must be coordinated. **Figure 4.5** shows a CD-ROM and an EIDE drive connected to a connector on the motherboard.

4. An EIDE disk drive requires an EIDE ribbon cable to connect it to the drive connector. If you are adding a second disk drive, you can use the existing cable as long as it has enough connectors.

5. Most computers these days will read all necessary drive parameters—cylinders, heads, sectors per track—from the drive, automatically. If for some reason this automatic process fails, you can enter the information manually. It should be printed on the drive (**Figure 4.6**) and probably in the drive documentation as well. If you can't find this information, check the drive manufacturer's Web site.

Master/slave settings for EIDE drives

An EIDE connector can support one or two EIDE devices. In order to communicate with the second device, your computer must first send a request to the first device, which then passes the information to the second. To keep things straight, one drive is set to be the *master* and the other is the *slave*. If there is only one device attached, then it is usually set to be a *single*, though some disk drives will work correctly as the master, even when they are alone.

Most systems come with two EIDE connectors. This means that there can be a maximum of four EIDE devices in the computer. If an EIDE CD-ROM drive is included, it is generally configured as the slave device on the second EIDE connector—it does not have to be the master device on its connector.

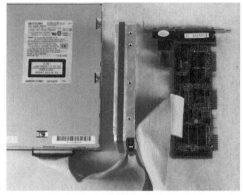

Figure 4.5 An EIDE disk drive and CD-ROM drive attached to a ribbon cable.

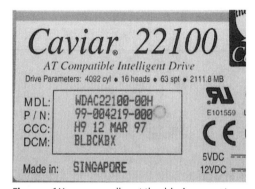

Figure 4.6 You can usually get the drive's parameters from a label on the disk drive itself.

Figure 4.7 Find the drive connector. It's attached via a ribbon cable to your existing hard drive.

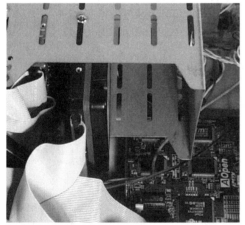

Figure 4.8 There should be a space for another hard drive next to your original drive.

✔ Tips

- It's a good idea not to put the CD-ROM drive on the same EIDE bus connector with a hard drive because the EIDE bus must slow down to the speed of the slowest device on the connector, which degrades the performance of the hard disk.

- When you are attaching the EIDE ribbon cable to the drives inside your computer, it doesn't matter in what order the drives are connected, as long as the motherboard connector is at one end of the cable.

Installing an EIDE hard drive

1. Unplug your computer, remove the screws from your case, and open the cover. Connect any anti-static devices you're using.

2. Find the EIDE drive connector. You can find it at the other end of the ribbon cable attached to the hard drive already in your PC (see **Figure 4.7**). If you do not have a disk drive in your computer already, look for two double rows of pins on the motherboard that match the connector on the EIDE ribbon cable. The pins are usually labeled "HDD 1" and "HDD 2," "EIDE 1" and "EIDE 2," or something similar.

3. The location for your new hard drive depends on the location of the drive connector. You must be able to reach the connector with the ribbon cable from the disk drive(s). Normally, there is room to install a second hard drive next to the first one, as illustrated in **Figure 4.8**.

4. Slide the new hard drive into the drive bay. This may be tricky if you have a small case and a lot of other wires and cables are in your way. Sometimes you can insert the hard drive from the front of the case by temporarily removing a spacing cover. In the worst case, you may have to

INSTALLING AN EIDE DRIVE

remove other adapter cards and unplug internal cables from the case to fit the drive into its new home.

In some cases, there will not be an empty drive bay that fits the width of your new hard disk. If you have a free bay that is wider than your drive, you can mount the drive by using drive rails. These rails may not be included with a new hard drive, but they are available at most computer stores.

The back of the disk drive—that is, the edge with the power and data connectors—should be facing into the computer case so that you can easily attach the ribbon cable and power lead (**Figure 4.9**), and the flywheel should be down. If you are adding a second disk drive, make sure you mount it with the power connector on the same side as the first drive.

5. Align the screw holes on the side of the hard drive with the holes on the side of the drive bay.

6. Fasten the hard drive into the drive bay with two screws, as in **Figure 4.10**. You don't need to use more screws, nor do you have to tighten them much more than finger-tight. These screws prevent the drive from slipping around inside the case when you move the PC and also keep the drive in contact with the grounded chassis.

7. Be careful: Some poorly designed disk drives risk damage to their printed circuit boards when the fastening screws are over-tightened. Never use screws that are too long.

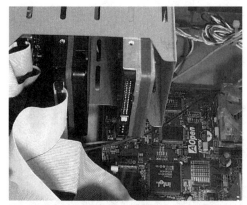

Figure 4.9 It can be a tight squeeze to insert the new drive. Make sure the connectors are facing the inside of the computer.

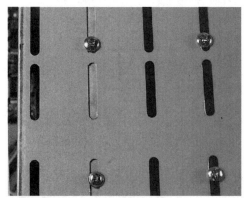

Figure 4.10 Insert a couple of screws to secure the new drive, but don't over-tighten.

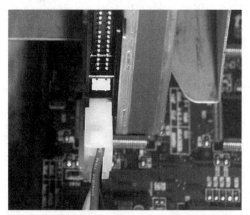

Figure 4.11 Connect the power lead to the disk drive, but don't force it in.

INSTALLING AN EIDE DRIVE

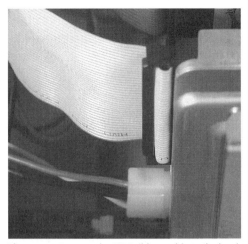

Figure 4.12 Connect the EIDE ribbon cable to the hard drive. Make sure the edge of the cable marked with a stripe is closest to the power socket on the drive.

Figure 4.13 When connecting the ribbon cable to the connector, be sure to line up the number-one pin correctly.

Making EIDE hard-drive connections

1. Connect a free power cable to the disk drive, as in **Figure 4.11**. The power cable will only fit into the power socket one way, so don't force it.

2. Connect the EIDE ribbon cable to the hard drive. One wire in the ribbon cable should be marked with a stripe or solid color. This is the *number-one wire*, and it should go to *pin one*—which is usually the pin closest to the power socket on the hard drive (**Figure 4.12**).

   If you are replacing a hard drive or adding a second one, one end of the ribbon cable should already be attached to the EIDE connector. Leave it connected. It doesn't matter in what order the two disk drives are attached to the other end of the cable.

   If you are installing a single disk drive, make sure that the other end of the EIDE cable is connected properly to the EIDE connector on the motherboard. The double row of pins on the connector should have a small arrow or numeral "1" printed nearby indicating pin one. Match that with the number one (red-striped) wire on the cable (**Figure 4.13**).

3. Leave the cover open while you complete the configuration, in case you have to fiddle around later. Incorrect master/slave settings or reverse ribbon connections won't permanently harm your hardware, but constantly opening and closing your case will certainly frustrate you.

INSTALLING AN EIDE DRIVE

Configuring the New EIDE Drive

After you've installed the hard drive, you must configure it in the PC's BIOS. Although this procedure may sound intimidating, it's actually not that bad if you take it step by step, and of course that's exactly what we are going to do. (For more on using the BIOS, see Chapter 2.)

EIDE hard drive BIOS configuration

1. Go into the system's Setup configuration menu. How you do this varies from computer to computer, but you'll most likely restart the machine and hit the Del key when the POST screen is displayed. If your PC does not indicate how to enter the BIOS setup menu when it boots, check your system or motherboard documentation.

2. Most setup routines are already configured to automatically detect hard drives. Look for a menu option such as "Auto detect HDD" or "HDD auto configuration" or "Auto" as shown in **Figure 4.14**. If it isn't enabled, enable it now. Save the changes and continue booting the computer. It should correctly identify the new hard drive.

   Some older computers will not automatically detect hard drives at start up, but will perform an auto-detect from a menu command in the BIOS setup menus.

   These days it's quite rare for a computer to lack hard drive auto-detection, but if by some chance your computer does not have this function, you'll have to set the disk parameters manually. (Also, in some cases the automatic hard-drive detection may not work. Though this is usually means the hard drive is installed incorrectly, you can still set the drive parame-

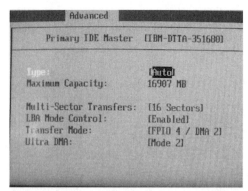

Figure 4.14 Most BIOS screens have an HDD Auto-configuration option.

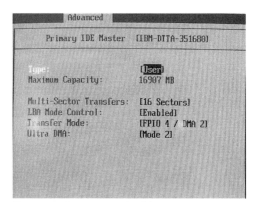

Figure 4.15 You can enter the drive parameters manually in the BIOS if you have to.

ters manually to confirm that the drive is not properly connected.)

3. The setup for the hard drive parameters is usually on the first screen in the BIOS menu. The parameters you will need to type in should be printed on the drive, and in the documentation.

4. After you enter the drive parameters, either automatically or manually, save your changes and exit the setup menu. The computer will reboot.

✔ Tip

■ If you're using an older computer, you may have to select a drive type from a list of pre-configured parameters. The last type in the list is normally blank, which allows you to enter parameters manually (**Figure 4.15**).

Installing a SCSI Drive

All things being equal, SCSI disk drives are generally more expensive than EIDE disk drives. They are also usually faster and easier to expand if you want to add another drive down the road.

SCSI pre-installation

1. Set the SCSI ID for the new disk drive. Every device on a SCSI chain requires a unique SCSI ID. If you want to boot from the new SCSI disk, you must give the disk a lower ID number than any other device— usually ID 0. If you are simply adding a disk, just make sure it has a unique ID number.

    You normally set the ID number by moving jumpers on the back of the drive, though some manufacturers use DIP switches or other means to set the ID. Check your drive documentation.

2. SCSI devices are connected to a SCSI controller via a SCSI ribbon cable. If you are adding a drive to an existing SCSI chain, make sure the existing SCSI cable has a connector for your new drive.

3. If you are adding an external SCSI hard drive to your system, then you need an external SCSI cable with the proper connector (see **Figure 4.16**) to attach from your SCSI controller to the cabinet of the external SCSI device.

Installing an internal SCSI drive

1. Unplug your computer, remove the screws from your case, and open the cover. Connect any anti-static devices you're using.

2. Find the SCSI controller. It should be at the end of the ribbon cable attached to the SCSI devices already in your PC (**Figure 4.17**). If you do not have any

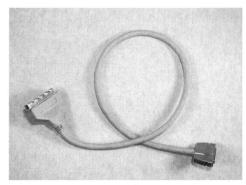

Figure 4.16 Several different SCSI connectors are available, so make sure you have what you need to complete the job.

Figure 4.17 Attach the SCSI ribbon cable to the SCSI controller card.

Figure 4.18 Make sure the drive connectors are facing the inside of the machine when you install the disk drive.

SCSI devices in your computer already, look for a double row of pins on an adapter card or on the motherboard that matches the connector on the SCSI ribbon cable.

3. Where you put your new hard drive depends on the location of the SCSI controller. You must be able to reach the SCSI connecter with the SCSI ribbon cable that's connected to the SCSI devices already in your system. Try to find a drive bay near the controller.

4. Slide the new hard drive into the drive bay—easier said than done if you have a small case and a lot of other wires and cables are in your way. Sometimes you can insert the hard drive from the front of the case by temporarily removing a spacing cover. In the worst case, you may have to remove other adapter cards and unplug internal cables from the case to fit the drive into its new home.

   The back of the disk drive—that is, the edge with the power and data connectors—should be facing into the computer case so that you can easily attach the ribbon cable and power lead, and the flywheel should be down, as in **Figure 4.18**.

5. Align the screw holes on the side of the hard drive with the holes on the side of the drive bay.

6. Fasten the hard drive into the drive bay with two screws; you won't need more than this, nor is it necessary to tighten the screws much more than finger-tight.

✔ Tip

■ Be careful: Some poorly designed disk drives risk damage to their printed circuit boards when the fastening screws are over-tightened. Never use screws that are too long.

INSTALLING A SCSI DRIVE

Internal SCSI hard drive connections

1. Connect a power cable to the disk drive, as in **Figure 4.19**. The cable only fits into the power socket one way, so don't force it.

2. Connect the SCSI ribbon cable to the hard drive as in **Figure 4.20**. One wire in the ribbon cable should be marked with a stripe or solid color. This is the number-one wire, and it goes to pin number one nearest the power socket on the hard drive. Install all hard drives with their power sockets on the same side so you won't have to twist the ribbon cable to connect multiple drives.

3. If you are adding a SCSI device to an existing chain, then one end of the ribbon cable should already be attached to the SCSI controller. If not, connect it now. The double row of pins on the controller should have a small arrow or numeral "1" printed nearby indicating pin one. Match that with the number one (red-striped) wire on the cable. Connect the rest of the devices to the SCSI cable.

4. You must terminate the last device on the SCSI chain. (See the section "SCSI hard drive configuration" later in this chapter for more info on SCSI termination.) On most SCSI hard drives, you attach resistors to the circuit board on the drive casing, as in **Figure 4.21**. Check your drive's documentation to find out how to terminate the drive correctly.

Figure 4.19 Connect the power cable to the disk drive. It only connects one way, so don't force it.

Figure 4.20 Connect the SCSI ribbon cable to the drive.

Figure 4.21 These are SCSI terminators.

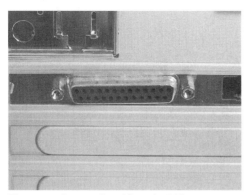

Figure 4.22 Connect the cable to the SCSI connector on the back of your computer.

Figure 4.23 You may have to set the termination by adjusting the jumpers on the SCSI controller.

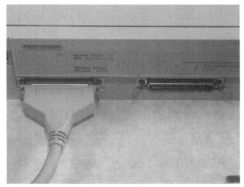

Figure 4.24 Connect the external SCSI cable so that the SCSI controller and the drive chassis are connected.

Installing an external SCSI drive

1. Make sure the computer is unplugged. You do not need to remove the cover. If you are adding the first external SCSI device to the PC, simply connect the cable to the connector on the back of your machine, as in **Figure 4.22**.

2. If you are adding the first external SCSI device to the PC, and *internal* SCSI devices are already installed, then you must configure the SCSI controller so that it is not terminated. Each SCSI controller is different, so consult your documentation for the correct jumper, DIP switch, or software utility that controls each item's termination. Often you must adjust jumpers to set termination, as in **Figure 4.23**.

3. If you are adding a new external disk drive to an existing external SCSI chain, unplug the existing SCSI cable from the external connector on the back of the PC. The new disk drive should be installed as the first physically connected device on the external SCSI chain, leaving the already-terminated device at the end.

4. Attach the external SCSI cable you just disconnected from the back of the PC to the connector on the back of the new hard drive chassis, as in **Figure 4.24**.

5. Attach one end of a new external SCSI cable to the external connector on the back of the PC. Attach the other end of the new external SCSI cable to the new disk drive. That's how you can chain SCSI drives together, as in **Figure 4.25**.

INSTALLING A SCSI DRIVE

75

SCSI drive configuration

1. Leave the computer case off if you had to open it to install an internal SCSI hard drive.

2. Power up the computer and watch after the POST screens for information about your new SCSI device.

   Unlike EIDE drives, SCSI drives do not need to be set up in the PC's BIOS. The SCSI controller has more logic built into it than an EIDE controller, making it smarter and easier to configure (and naturally more expensive).

3. The controller should automatically find the new SCSI hard drive you added when you reboot the computer. If it does not, then you may have a termination problem or a SCSI device ID conflict. Turn off the computer, double-check your device settings, and try booting the computer again.

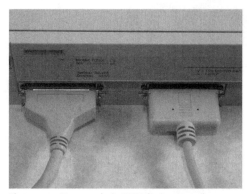

Figure 4.25 You can chain SCSI devices together.

About SCSI

SCSI has evolved over the years, and though it is mostly backward-compatible (works with older machines), you should consider some factors before buying new SCSI gear.

The controller and the drives must be of the same SCSI specification (SCSI-2, Fast SCSI, Fast Wide SCSI, etc.) to get maximum performance from the system. Otherwise, the slowest component will dictate performance. Also, the connectors for different specifications of SCSI are not all the same, but you can get adapters.

The SCSI chain must be properly terminated at both ends. This means that the last device at each physical end of the cable must provide termination. Generally, the SCSI controller terminates its end, and the last device on the chain terminates its end. If you have a combination of internal and external SCSI devices attached to the same controller, then the controller should not be terminated. Instead, the last device on the internal chain and the last device on the external chain are terminated. Your hard drive documentation will tell you how to terminate correctly.

Figure 4.26 When in MS-DOS, type **FDISK** at the prompt.

Partitioning the New SCSI Drive

Before you can use your new hard drive, you must create a partition on it for a file system and then format the partition.

If you are installing a primary hard drive in your computer, then you must also install an operating system on it before you can use it. We step you through the process in the following sections.

If you are adding a second disk drive to your PC, you don't need to install an operating system to use the new drive. However, you must still partition and format it. This procedure is different in each operating system, so check the documentation for your OS. If you use Windows 95 or 98, follow these steps.

Creating a partition on a second hard drive with FDISK

Warning: Changes made with the FDISK program are permanent. If you delete anything using FDISK, you will never, ever, ever get it back. There is no undo and no cancel feature. Check everything twice before making changes with FDISK!

1. Turn on the computer and let it boot into Windows 95/98.

2. Open a DOS session. You'll probably do this by clicking the Start button, opening the Programs menu, and clicking on the MS-DOS Prompt item.

3. At the DOS prompt, type **FDISK**, as in **Figure 4.26**.

    The file system in most versions of Windows 95 will only allow you to create partitions with a maximum size of 2 gigabytes. If your new disk drive is bigger than 2 GB, you will have to create multiple 2GB partitions in order to use all of the space. These partitions will each show up as a different drive letter.

Windows 98 is smarter than Windows 95—smart enough to create a partition as big as your hard disk. There is no 2 GB size limit in Windows 98. Windows 98 will ask if you want to enable large disk support, as in **Figure 4.27**. This option enables the FAT32 file system, which can use all of a large disk drive as one drive letter.

Selecting the correct physical drive in FDISK

1. At the FDISK Options menu choose item 5 to switch to the new hard drive (**Figure 4.28**). FDISK will display a list of the physical drives in the system.

2. Select the second physical drive—this should be the one you just installed. If you added a third or fourth drive, then select accordingly, as in **Figure 4.29**.

3. To confirm that you have the correct drive, choose item 4 at the FDISK Options menu. The hard disk should be empty of partitions. However, if you have installed a previously used disk drive, then you may see partition information that was left on it. Make a note of this information if you want to delete it (see the next section for more on deleting).

Deleting existing partitions in FDISK

1. With the correct drive as the current drive, select item 3 on the FDISK Options menu to bring up the "Delete DOS Partition or the Logical DOS Drive" (**Figure 4.30**) menu.

There are two kinds of partitions that you can have in FAT16 and FAT32 file systems. A *primary* partition allows you to boot your computer and is not subdivided any further. An *extended* parti-

Figure 4.27 You will probably want to say Yes to this prompt, especially if your disk size is larger than 512 MB.

Figure 4.28 Selecting option 5 in the FDISK Options menu will display a list of physical disk drives in your system.

Figure 4.29 Select the drive in question from the menu.

Figure 4.30 Use the Delete menu in FDISK to get rid of those pesky partitions.

Figure 4.31 Once the partitions have been deleted, you'll get this confirmation.

Figure 4.32 Select item 1 in the Create DOS Partition menu to create a new partition.

Partition This!

We recommend that you partition your hard drive into one large partition. If you do not have a version of Windows 95/98 that supports the 32-bit FAT file system, then you will have to break your greater-than-2-GB hard drive into smaller partitions. This may be just the incentive you need to upgrade to Windows 98.

tion is usually created after the primary partition and may be sub-divided into more than one logical drive.

2. If you find logical DOS drives in an extended partition on the disk drive, you must delete them before the extended partition can be deleted. Select item 3 in the FDISK Delete menu.

If no logical drives exist you will see a warning message and be returned to the FDISK Options menu. Skip the next step.

3. At the Delete Logical DOS drive screen, choose the logical drive to delete. Continue steps two, three, and four until all logical drives are gone (**Figure 4.31**).

4. To delete a primary or extended partition, select the appropriate item in the FDISK Delete menu.

5. Now you're ready to add your own partition.

Creating hard disk partitions with FDISK

1. Run FDISK in a DOS session. If it is already running, return to the FDISK Options menu.

2. Confirm that you have the correct hard drive selected as the current fixed disk drive. If not, select menu item 5 and choose the correct physical drive.

3. Select menu item 1 to create a DOS partition.

4. At the FDISK Create DOS Partition menu, select item 1 to create a primary partition, as in **Figure 4.32**.

5. FDISK will ask you if you want to use the entire disk capacity for the primary partition. We recommend that you do so. If you do not, then you will have to specify a percentage of the disk drive for the primary partition.

PARTITIONING THE NEW SCSI DRIVE

6. After FDISK has created the partition, it will verify the integrity of the drive, which may take up to several minutes on large drives. When it finishes, you can press Esc until the program exits. FDISK will warn you to reboot your computer so the changes take effect.

7. When the computer restarts you will have a new drive letter available—but you're not quite ready to use it yet! Read on...

Formatting a drive in Windows 95/98

1. The operating system must format your new hard drive before you can use it. Double-click on the My Computer icon on your desktop to open the My Computer window, as in **Figure 4.33**.

2. Find the new drive and right-click on it to open the pop-up menu. The new drive should give you an error message when you try to double-click on it because it is not yet formatted.

3. Select Format from the pop-up menu.

4. A warning message tells you that formatting this fixed disk will remove any existing information **Figure 4.34**). This warning pops up whether any information is on the disk or not, so don't worry—just make very, very certain that the disk you are formatting is the new one.

5. In the Format dialog box you should select a full format and type in a volume label if you want (**Figure 4.35**). (The label can be changed later, so you don't have to specify one now.)

6. After the format is completed, Windows suggests that you run a complete surface scan of the drive. Go ahead and do this—especially if you have installed a previously used drive. See the next section to find out how.

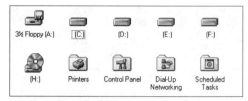

Figure 4.33 Double click on the My Computer icon on your desktop to get here.

Figure 4.34 You'll get this warning whether there's data on the disk or not. Just make sure you're erasing the right disk!

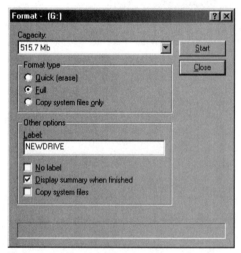

Figure 4.35 Select a full format and give each drive a name.

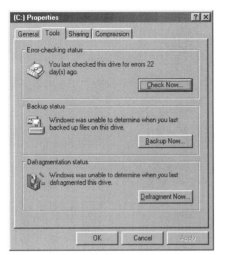

Figure 4.36 Select the Tools tab in the Drive Properties dialog window.

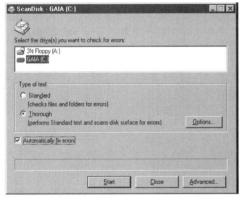

Figure 4.37 Be sure to select the correct drive letter in the Scandisk dialog window.

Running a surface scan on a disk drive

1. Open the My Computer icon to start the My Computer interface.

2. Right-click the drive icon of the new drive letter you have just added.

3. Select Properties from the pop-up menu.

4. Select the Tools tab, as in **Figure 4.36**, at the top of the Drive Properties dialog window.

5. Click the Check Now button in the Error-checking status section.

6. Select the correct drive letter in the Scandisk dialog window (**Figure 4.37**).

7. Select the Thorough radio button, click the "Automatically fix errors" check box, and click the Start button on the window. This process will run for a long time—as long as an hour—so you may want to leave it and come back in a while.

   If there are any problems, you will see an error message telling you what was found. If your brand-new disk drive has errors on it, you should return it. If everything checks out, then you can start using your new hard drive.

Replacing Your Primary Hard Drive

The steps for replacing the primary hard drive in your computer are similar to installing a second drive. The procedure is more complicated, though, because of the extra steps involved in moving information from your existing drive to the new one.

The very safest way to replace your primary drive is to back up the old drive, install your new drive, format it, transfer an operating system onto it, reload Windows and your applications on it from the original installation disks, and then restore your data. However, in most cases the procedure outlined in the following section offers a reasonably reliable and much faster alternative.

✔ Tip

- There are products available that make this "system transfer" procedure simpler. Symantec Ghost is an excellent package that will help you transfer your system to a new disk drive quickly and safely. Check it out on the Symantec Web site (www.symantec.com) before you do the hard drive shuffle.

Replacing the drive

1. Do a complete backup of the entire contents of the hard disk(s) in your PC. When the backup is complete, verify it. We cannot stress too highly how important this step is!

2. If you don't already have an up-to-date Windows start-up diskette, create one now.

    In the Control Panel, double-click the Add/Remove Programs icon and click the Startup Disk tab. Insert a blank diskette and click the Create Disk button to continue.

After the start-up diskette has been created, reboot your computer with this new diskette to make sure it works.

Turn off the PC, unplug it, open it up, and install the new hard disk temporarily as a slave to your existing hard drive. This will probably involve changing the jumpers on both hard drives. See the sections earlier in this chapter called "Preparing to install an EIDE hard drive" and "Installing an EIDE hard drive."

Remember, you are temporarily installing the new drive as the second drive, so it should be the slave device.

4. When the new drive is physically installed, start your computer and go into the BIOS setup menu to confirm that the new drive is properly detected. See the section "EIDE hard drive BIOS configuration" earlier in this chapter.

5. Reboot your computer from the start-up disk.

6. Run FDISK and partition the new drive. Make sure you create a *primary* partition, not an *extended* partition. See the section "Creating hard disk partitions with FDISK" earlier in this chapter. You will have to reboot your computer (from the start-up disk) for the changes to take effect.

7. Format the new drive. Check the drive letter to make very, very certain that you are formatting the new drive, and not an existing drive with data on it. When you format the new drive, include the system files so that the computer can boot from it later. See the section "Formatting a drive in Windows 95/98" earlier in this chapter.

8. Now you need to copy your existing drive onto the new drive. Follow these instructions exactly. From the DOS prompt, type this command:

```
XCOPY C:\*.* D:\*.* /E /C /H /K
```

In this example, we assume that your new drive letter is D: and your old drive letter is C:. If your drive letter setup is different, substitute your correct drive letters.

During the copy process you will get an error message when the PC tries to copy the Windows swap file. This error is not a cause for concern. The copying process may take as long as 30 minutes, depending on the size of your current primary drive.

9. Shut down your computer and switch the master/slave configuration of your hard disks so that the new drive is now the master. If you do not want to leave your old hard disk in you can remove it.

   Important: Do not erase or change any data on your old hard disk until you are confident that your new disk has been working properly and perfectly for at least a week.

10. Insert your start-up floppy disk in the disk drive and start your computer—but before the operating system boots, go into the BIOS setup menu by pressing the Del button. Confirm that your BIOS has auto-detected the new disk drive as the first or only hard disk.

11. Continue booting your computer from the start-up disk. At the DOS prompt, type **FDISK** and set the primary partition on the new hard drive to be the active partition. This is menu item 2 in the FDISK options screen.

12. If everything has gone correctly, you should now be able to remove the start-up diskette and boot your computer from the new hard disk. Windows should start normally, and all of your settings, icons, applications, and data should be just where they were before you swapped disk drives.

If you have any problems with this procedure, you can always return to the slow, safe way: Re-install Windows from the Windows installation CD and then re-install any applications that are not working properly.

Here's what the command described in step 8 of the preceding section means:

XCOPY: Copies files and directories.

C:*.*: Specifies the source files to copy.

D:*.*: Specifies the destination.

/E: Copies directories and subdirectories even if they are empty.

/C: Continues copying if an error occurs.

/H: Copies hidden and system files.

/K: Copies the files attributes instead of resetting them.

REPLACING YOUR PRIMARY HARD DRIVE

Installing a CD-ROM or DVD-ROM Drive

Adding a CD-ROM or DVD-ROM drive to your PC is similar to installing a hard drive. The only differences are that there are some extra connections to make and fewer config-uration issues to worry about.

CD-ROMs are available for the PC as SCSI devices, but EIDE CD-ROM drives are far more common. EIDE devices are cheaper and easier to configure, and because most PCs already have an EIDE hard drive, it is a simple matter to add an EIDE CD-ROM drive to the system. SCSI CD-ROM drives are a lit-tle more complicated because you have to deal with ID numbers and make sure the SCSI bus is properly terminated.

Figure 4.38 Set the jumpers on the CD-ROM to make it a slave drive.

EIDE CD-ROM and DVD-ROM drive pre-installation

1. Set the drive to be an EIDE slave device. Do this with jumpers or DIP switches (**Figure 4.38**), depending on the drive; check the documentation to make sure.

   Although a CD-ROM will work on the first or second EIDE connector, CD-ROM drives are usually configured as the slave device on the second EIDE connector. This leaves the first EIDE connector for hard drives, and you can still add a third disk drive without having to reconfigure the CD-ROM.

2. If you are installing the CD-ROM drive into a system that already has a hard drive on the second EIDE controller, the disk drive will have to be set to be a mas-ter device if it isn't already. Consult the hard drive's documentation for the neces-sary jumper or DIP switch settings.

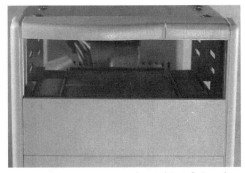

Figure 4.39 Most CD-ROM and DVD drives fit into the 5.25-inch drive bays.

Figure 4.40 Remove the plastic spacer in the front of your PC so that you can easily insert the CD/DVD drive.

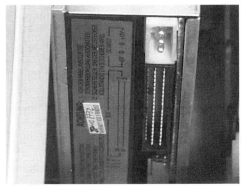

Figure 4.41 Be sure to install the CD/DVD drive so that the connectors are facing the machine's innards.

3. You may need an EIDE ribbon cable to connect the CD-ROM drive to the controller. If you already have a drive connected to the second connector with an EIDE cable, that cable will probably have a connector for the new CD-ROM device.

Installing EIDE CD-ROM and DVD-ROM drives

1. Make sure your computer is unplugged. Remove the screws from your case and open the cover. Connect any anti-static devices you are using.

2. Where your new CD-ROM drive goes depends on your case. CD and DVD drives are almost always 5.25 inches wide, as shown in **Figure 4.39**. Small cases may have only one drive bay wide enough for the drive. Obviously, the drive bay must be external, with an opening to the front of the computer case, since you'll need to insert and remove CD-ROM disks while operating your computer.

3. You must be able to reach the new CD-ROM drive with an EIDE ribbon cable from the EIDE connector. If the cable you have is too short, you can buy a longer one at most computer stores.

4. Slide the new CD-ROM drive into the drive bay. You'll find it easiest to insert the drive from the front of the case by removing the spacing cover (**Figure 4.40**). You probably won't need the spacer any more, but keeping extra pieces might be a good idea in the event that you remove the drive someday.

The back of the drive should be facing into the computer case so that you can easily attach the ribbon cable and power lead, shown in **Figure 4.41**.

5. Align the screw holes on the side of the CD-ROM drive with the holes on the side of the drive bay.

6. Fasten the drive into the drive bay with at least two screws. New CD-ROM and DVD-ROM drives normally come with four screws, but you don't need them all. Tighten the screws firmly, but don't force them. A CD-ROM drive needs to be locked down a bit more firmly than a hard drive because the in-out sliding action of the disk tray can wiggle it out of position. But you can damage the drive if you over-tighten the screws.

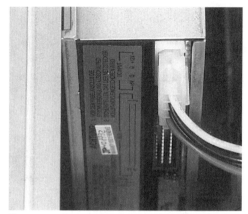

Figure 4.42 Connect the power lead to the CD/DVD drive.

EIDE CD-ROM and DVD-ROM drive connections

1. Connect a power cable to the new drive, as in **Figure 4.42**. The cable will only fit into the power socket one way, so don't force it.

2. Connect the EIDE ribbon cable to the CD-ROM drive. One wire in the ribbon cable should be marked with a stripe or solid color. This is the number-one wire, and it goes to pin number one, nearest to the power socket on the drive.

3. If you are adding a CD-ROM drive to an EIDE connector that already has a hard drive attached, then one end of the ribbon cable should already be connected to the EIDE connector. It doesn't matter in what order the two drives are attached to the cable (**Figure 4.43**).

4. If you are installing a CD-ROM drive as the only device on the second connector, make sure that the other end of the EIDE cable is connected securely to the connector. The double row of pins on the controller should have a small arrow or numeral "1" printed nearby indicating pin one. Connect the red-striped edge of the cable to this pin.

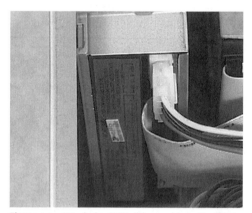

Figure 4.43 Attach the EIDE ribbon cable to the EIDE controller.

Figure 4.44 This is the audio cable connection for CD-ROM drives.

Figure 4.45 The CD audio cable attaches to the sound card.

Figure 4.46 The DVD-ROM requires an MPEG video cable.

5. CD-ROM and DVD-ROM drives require an audio cable to be connected from the CD audio output on the back of the drive to the CD audio input pins on your sound card. This connector is shown in **Figure 4.44**. If by some chance the cable provided with the drive does not match the pins on your sound board, the sound board manufacturer can provide you with the correct cable.

   The audio output connector on the back of the CD-ROM or DVD-ROM drive should be labeled, but you can check the drive manual if it isn't. The connector on the sound card is usually labeled "CD Audio" or simply "CD," as in **Figure 4.45**. If not, check the sound card documentation.

6. Some DVD-ROM drives come with an MPEG-2 decoder adapter card. This card fits into an expansion slot in your computer. It may require a cable connected inside the case to your video card (see **Figure 4.46**), or it may use a "pass-through" cable that connects the output from the back of your video card to an input on the back of the MPEG-2 decoder card. In such a case, the monitor cable is connected to the output on the back of the MPEG-2 decoder card.

   The documentation that came with your DVD-ROM drive and MPEG-2 decoder board will explain how to make all the connections. Contact the manufacturer if you have further questions.

7. Leave the case open while you complete the configuration. Incorrect master/slave settings or reverse ribbon connections will not permanently harm your hardware, but will probably prevent the system from booting properly—and in any case you don't want to keep re-opening the case to make corrections.

SCSI CD-ROM and DVD-ROM drive pre-installation

1. Select the SCSI ID number for the new device by changing jumpers or DIP switches, depending on the drive; check the documentation that came with it. You must choose an ID number that is not being used by any other device on that SCSI chain.

2. If you are installing an external CD-ROM or DVD-ROM, and there are no other external devices attached to your SCSI controller, then you will have to remove the termination from your SCSI controller. Depending on the controller, this is done with jumpers or a utility program. You will need your SCSI adapter card documentation.

3. You may need a new internal SCSI ribbon cable to connect the CD-ROM drive to the controller and other devices if the current cable does not have enough connectors.

SCSI CD-ROM and DVD-ROM drive installation

1. Make sure your computer is unplugged. Remove the screws from your case and open the cover if you are installing an internal drive, or if you need to access the SCSI controller card to change the termination setting. Connect any anti-static devices you are using.

2. Where your new internal CD-ROM drive goes depends on your case. CD and DVD drives are almost always 5.25 inches wide (refer back to **Figure 4.39**). Small cases may have only one drive bay wide enough for the drive. Obviously, the drive bay must be external, with an opening to the front of the computer case, since you'll need to insert and remove CD-ROM disks while operating your computer.

If you are adding an external drive, then you should place the CD-ROM or DVD-ROM drive close to any other external SCSI devices connected to your system. This makes connecting them easier.

3. You must be able to reach the new internal CD-ROM drive with the SCSI ribbon cable that's connected to the SCSI devices already in your system. For external drives, it is easiest to connect the new drive to the SCSI adapter, then connect the rest of your external SCSI devices to the new drive. That way you don't have to terminate the new drive.

4. For internal drives, slide the CD-ROM drive into the drive bay. You'll find that it's easiest to insert the drive from the front of the case by removing the spacing cover (shown back in **Figure 4.40**).

   The back of the drive should be facing into the computer case so that you can easily attach the SCSI ribbon cable and power lead.

5. Align the screw holes on the side of the internal CD-ROM drive with the holes on the side of the drive bay.

6. Fasten the internal drive into the drive bay with at least two screws. New CD-ROM and DVD-ROM drives normally come with four screws, but you don't need them all. Tighten the screws firmly, but don't force them.

SCSI CD-ROM and DVD-ROM drive connections

1. Connect a power cable to the new internal drive. The cable will only fit into the power socket one way, so don't force it. External drives plug directly into a wall outlet—but do not make this connection yet!

2. Connect the SCSI ribbon cable to the internal CD-ROM drive. One wire in the

ribbon cable should be marked with a stripe or solid color. This is the number-one wire, and it goes to pin number 1 nearest to the power socket on the drive.

External SCSI CD-ROMs are connected to other SCSI devices in a daisy-chain link. It is easiest to connect the new device directly to the SCSI controller and then attach the existing devices to the new device so that you do not have to terminate the new drive. Follow the procedure outlined above for installing an external SCSI hard drive.

3. If you are installing a CD-ROM drive as the only device on the SCSI controller, then it must be terminated. This applies to internal and external drives. Connect the SCSI cable from the controller to the drive.

4. CD-ROM and DVD-ROM drives require an additional cable—an audio cable—to be connected from the CD audio output on the back of the drive to the CD audio input pins on your sound card. If by some chance the cable provided with the drive does not match the pins on your sound board, the sound board manufacturer can provide you with the correct cable.

   The audio output connector on the back of the CD-ROM or DVD-ROM drive should be labeled, but you can check the drive manual if it isn't.

5. Some DVD-ROM drives come with an MPEG-2 decoder adapter card. This card fits into an expansion slot in your computer. It may require a cable connected inside the case to your video card, or may use a "pass-through" cable that connects the output from the back of your video card to an input on the back of the MPEG-2 decoder card. In this case, the monitor cable is connected to the output on the back of the MPEG-2 decoder card.

Figure 4.47 Windows configures the new drive.

The documentation that came with your DVD-ROM drive and MPEG-2 decoder board will explain how to make all the connections. Contact the manufacturer if you have further questions.

6. Leave the case open while you complete the configuration so you don't keep re-opening the case to make corrections.

After you install the drive, the next step is to set up the new hardware so that the operating system can use it. CD-ROM and DVD-ROM drives do not need to be configured in the computer's BIOS, though you may see a message each time you boot your computer that the new drive has been detected. Newer computers will list the disk devices, Plug N Play adapters, and PCI resources that they detect during the POST procedure.

Configuring a CD-ROM or DVD-ROM drive

1. Turn on your computer and let it boot into Windows.

2. Let Windows detect the new CD-ROM or DVD-ROM drive, as seen in **Figure 4.47**.

3. Windows may ask you for a driver disk. If it does, insert the diskette that came with your CD-ROM drive and follow the on-screen prompts to complete installation.

If all is well, you can power down your PC, replace the cover, and reboot the machine to start enjoying your CD-ROM or DVD-ROM drive. If all is not well, check and follow the troubleshooting procedures outlined in Chapter 2.

INSTALLING A CD-ROM OR DVD-ROM DRIVE

✔ Tips

- It is important to note that the old IDE drive controllers can't handle CD-ROM or DVD-ROM drives. This feature was added as part of the EIDE specification, so systems with an IDE drive controller must be upgraded to EIDE or SCSI.

- The audio cable is a slim wire with two or three wires inside. If you find that the connectors on the ends will not fit either your CD-ROM or the sound card, you might be able to get a replacement CD audio cable at a local computer store. Write down the brand name of your CD-ROM drive and sound card before you go searching. Better yet, contact the CD-ROM drive vendor or sound board vendor for a replacement cable.

- If you do not install the CD audio cable, your CD-ROM or DVD-ROM drive will still function correctly while reading discs, and will play some audio files—but it won't be able to play CD audio properly.

VIDEO
DISPLAY DEVICES

5

Many PCs, especially older ones, were originally outfitted with cutting-edge video cards. But with the passing years, those cards are no longer able to keep up with today's higher resolutions and larger monitors.

A state-of-the-art video card isn't exactly a must-have piece of equipment, but just on general principle, if your current display adapter is more than two years old, you should probably think about upgrading to a newer one. And if you use any video or graphics applications, and especially if you're an avid gamer, a snazzy video card is less of a luxury and more of a necessity.

Chapter 5

About Video Cards

Screen *resolution* describes how many points of light (called *pixels*) are displayed on the screen. The more pixels, the more detail that can be shown. Standard VGA resolution is 640 x 480 pixels. Modern Windows applications are often designed for higher resolutions than 640 x 480—resolutions that weren't widely supported even a few years ago.

If toolbars, status bars, and Help windows are taking up so much of the screen that there's hardly room for your data, or if you'd like to see more of your application at a time, you should switch to a higher screen resolution, such as 800 x 600 or 1024 x 768. But note: An outdated video card may not let you do that (more on this later in this chapter).

Color depth is a way of describing how many colors can be displayed on the screen at the same time. Most people who spend time surfing the Internet or trading digital family snapshots will notice that the pictures do not look quite right unless they are viewed at a color depth of at least 16,384 colors (also referred to as 16-bit color depth). Fewer colors than this will distort the hues and color tones in the image. Therefore, having a modern video card is important for Internet surfers.

Color depth and resolution both require video memory, and if your card is under-endowed with video memory you will have to choose between higher resolutions and higher color depth. For instance, an outdated video card may not have enough video memory to display 16-bit color at 1024 x 768 resolution.

Video cards today should have a minimum of 8 MB of video RAM. The amount of video RAM in the card limits the highest screen resolution and the color depth at that resolution. Let's do some quick math:

640x480x8-bit color = 307,200 bytes

640x480x16-bit color = 614,400 bytes

640x480x32-bit color = 1,228,800 bytes

800x600x8-bit color = 480,000 bytes

800x600x16-bit color = 960,000 bytes

800x600x32-bit color = 1,920,000 bytes

1024x768x8-bit color = 786,432 bytes

1024x768x16-bit color = 1,572,864 bytes

1024x768x32-bit color = 3,145,728 bytes

1280x1024x8-bit color = 1,310,720 bytes

1280x1024x16-bit color = 2,621,440 bytes

1280x1024x32-bit color = 5,242,880 bytes

As the monitors on the market get bigger and better, screen resolutions get higher. It is common to use a screen resolution of 1024x768 pixels at 32-bit color depth. And as you can see, that setup requires a video card with 3.15 MB of video RAM. Because video cards only come with an even amount of RAM, you'll need a 4 MB card to support this display mode. If your video card does not have enough memory, then Windows will not let you switch to that screen mode.

Extra RAM on the video card is used as a buffer to store extra video information. This speeds up the display quite a bit.

Computer games use video RAM for the *texture cache* in 3D video games. The texture cache makes it possible to draw an image very quickly. The newest type of video card— AGP cards—can use the main system memory as a texture cache area so they do not need as much video memory.

The best video cards available today feature extra instructions that speed up the display of 3D computer games (and other 3D applications like rendering and drawing tools). If you ever play 3D games on your computer, then a 3D accelerator video card will make a world of difference.

Other features on modern video cards include video inputs and outputs, TV tuners, and MPEG decoders. This last feature allows you to watch DVD movies on your computer (or on your TV if your video card has a video-out port) if you have a DVD drive installed.

Your video card's *refresh rate* directly affects your eyes; a low rate produces a visible flicker; a high rate makes those late nights in front of your computer much easier. A video card that can output at a refresh rate of 72 Hz or more may reduce eye strain and help prevent headaches and other physical discomforts. In general, the higher the resolution, the lower the refresh rate your video card can produce. You'll have to pay more for a video card that gives you higher refresh rates at higher resolutions, but we think it's worth the cost.

More and more movies and software are becoming available in DVD format, a format that will probably be virtually ubiquitous in a few years. But you need an MPEG-2 decoder (either software or hardware) to view DVD video. Some video cards provide hardware decoding of MPEG-2 video, either on the board itself or through a plug-in expansion card that attaches to the video card or goes in a separate slot. You can buy an MPEG-2 decoder board separately at any time, but if you're upgrading your video board you should consider getting one that supports MPEG-2 decoding.

If you have a fast computer, 300MHz or better, software MPEG-2 decoding will work about as well as hardware, but if you intend to watch the DVD output on your television (as opposed to your computer monitor), you will get a much better TV image from a hardware MPEG-2 decoder card.

Video Cards for Gamers

Video cards that accelerate the display of 3D games and graphics are extremely popular. If you're a gamer, you should consider this feature when you're shopping around for a video card. For specific information, see the section "3D accelerator cards" later in this chapter.

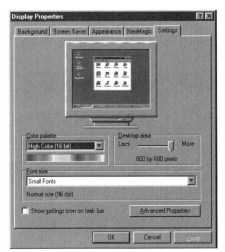

Figure 5.1 The Windows 98 Display Properties dialog box shows you the standard VGA video drivers installed.

Figure 5.2 Empty PCI slots for a video card. Your new video card will slide into one of these.

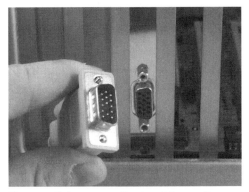

Figure 5.3 Make sure you disconnect the monitor cable before you try to remove the old video card.

Installing a Video Card

Physically installing a new video card in your PC is fairly easy. The software configuration may cause you some problems, but we'll guide you through the entire process.

Video card pre-installation

1. Presumably, your PC already has a video card. Before yanking it out, boot your computer and set the display drivers to plain VGA (**Figure 5.1**). (See the section "Changing Windows display drivers" later in this chapter.)

2. Windows 95/98 can detect and configure a wide range of video cards automatically, but it's much better to use the display drivers provided by the video card manufacturer on a floppy diskette or a CD-ROM. So, when you are offered a choice between using a Windows driver and the manufacturer's driver, use the manufacturer's.

3. Most video cards sold today are designed to fit a PCI or AGP slot, as in **Figure 5.2**. Make sure you know which kind of slot your new video card requires and that you have one available. Older computers use either ISA or VESA slots for their video boards, but it's becoming harder and harder to find video boards designed to fit those slots. If your PC requires an ISA or VESA video board, you should consider buying a new PC.

Video card installation

1. Make sure your PC is unplugged and then open the case.

2. Unplug the video cable (the one attached to your monitor) from the connector on your existing video card (**Figure 5.3**).

3. Remove the video card by unscrewing the single screw from the bracket that holds the card in the case.

4. Pull out the card. You may need to rock it back and forth to loosen it from the slot.

5. Most likely you will be placing your new board in the same slot. (If not, find an empty bus slot of the same type as your new video card.) In either case, fit the card into the slot (**Figure 5.4**). Make sure it is seated properly—the metal tabs that slide into the slot should be almost totally hidden inside the slot.

6. Fasten the adapter card to the case with the bracket screw.

7. Attach the monitor cable to the new video card (see **Figure 5.5**).

8. Leave the case open, in case the configuration process reveals any problems.

Multisync monitors and your video card

Your video card and monitor must both be set to use the same display frequency. If your monitor does not support the refresh rate and resolution that your video board puts out, you'll get a corrupted video image or none at all. Fortunately, most monitors sold in the past few years are *multifrequency* (also known as *multisynch* and *multiscan*) units that automatically synch to the refresh rate put out by the video card.

Check your monitor's specifications before spending a lot of money on a video card that your monitor won't be able to keep up with. If necessary, you can usually set the video card to use a lower refresh rate in the Windows Display Properties dialog. See the section "Configuring video card software in Windows 95/98" later in this chapter.

Figure 5.4 A PCI video card fits into the adapter slot on the motherboard.

Figure 5.5 To find the video card, match the VGA connector on the back of a video card with the cable to your monitor.

Display Drivers

Display drivers are software programs that tell the operating system how to send information to the video card. Each video card has a unique display driver, but every video card should work in a limited fashion with the VGA driver.

Figure 5.6 After Windows 98 detects new hardware, you will go to the Update Device Driver Wizard.

Video Card Software

Installing a video card is only half the battle; next you have to install the video driver. Windows 95/98 comes with many generic video drivers that will probably work with your new card, but the one that comes with your video card is best.

Configuring video card software

1. Turn on your computer. If you see the normal start-up information on your monitor, then the video-card hardware is probably correctly installed. If the screen is blank, and you hear a series of beeps, check to make sure that your video card is seated properly in its slot and that the monitor cable is properly connected to the card. If these steps still don't help, then you may have a defective video card.

2. Allow Windows to start. Your display may look strange, because you'll be using a standard VGA resolution of 640 x 480 pixels. You'll have to install the proper display drivers to use your card's extended capabilities.

3. Windows will probably detect your new video card and ask you to insert the driver disk (see **Figure 5.6**). Insert the CD-ROM or diskette that contains the manufacturer's video drivers and select the correct drive letter and directory in the Windows driver dialog box. Often the CD-ROM or diskette will have several directories with video drivers for different operating systems. You should select the Windows 95 or Windows 98 directory. If you are using Windows 98, and there is only a Windows 95 directory, try the drivers there.

4. After the new driver is loaded, and Windows has re-started properly, you can adjust your monitor's resolution and

refresh rate by double clicking the Display icon (**Figure 5.7**) in the Control Panels folder (under Settings in the Start menu).

5. In the Display Properties dialog, click the Settings tab. This tab lets you pick the screen resolution and color depth. Click the Advanced button to adjust the video refresh rate.

Video card vendors are constantly updating their video drivers. You can usually find new drivers for your video card on the manufacturer's Web site. Be sure to read all notes and documentation provided with the new drivers *before* you install them. After you download the drivers, you normally have to extract them to a directory or diskette before you can continue.

Changing Windows' display drivers

1. Open the Display Properties dialog window by opening the Windows Control Panel and double-clicking the Display icon, or by right-clicking anywhere on your desktop and selecting Properties from the pop-up menu.

2. Select the tab labeled Settings, as shown in **Figures 5.8** (Windows 95) and **5.9** (Windows 98).

3. In Windows 95 you can change the video display driver by clicking the Advanced Properties button (**Figure 5.10**). In the earliest version of Windows 95, however, there is no such button. You can simply click the Change button beside the name of the current display driver and skip the next step (**Figure 5.11**). Windows 98 has the same button, but it is labeled "Advanced...".

The Advanced Display Properties dialog box shows the current display driver under the Adapter tab.

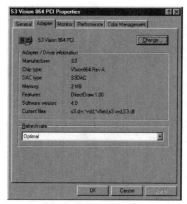

Figure 5.7 The Display Properties window shows the current refresh rate.

Figure 5.8 The Windows 98 Display Properties window shows the Settings tab.

Figure 5.9 Windows 95's Display Properties window shows the Settings tab.

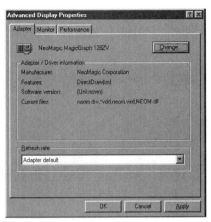

Figure 5.10 Windows 98's Advanced Display Properties dialog window.

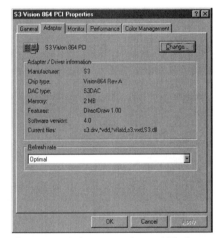

Figure 5.11 Windows 95's Advanced Display Properties dialog.

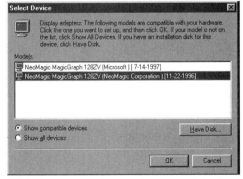

Figure 5.12 The Windows 95 Select Device dialog box.

4. Click the Change button beside the name of the current display driver. The Select Device dialog box opens to show you a list of the compatible display drivers that Windows thinks are appropriate.

5. Either click the Show All Devices button (**Figure 5.12**) to pick from Windows' list of display drivers or click the Have Disk... button to locate a set of drivers you may have on a disk or CD-ROM or downloaded into a folder.

6. After you select a driver, Windows will copy files to the system directories and then reboot.

VIDEO CARD SOFTWARE

✔ Tip

■ It is always preferable to install the drivers provided by the video card manufacturer. The only time you'd want to install the generic Windows drivers is if you are having a problem with the current video drivers and you want to confirm that it is a driver problem. The video display drivers provided by Windows will usually allow you to use your video card's full resolution and refresh rate, but the manufacturer's drivers usually include extra settings that let you tweak the display to your exact preferences. These may include color adjustment, a virtual desktop, or other options that let you increase the performance of your hardware. In many cases, advanced features like video-out and MPEG-2 decoding are not available unless you use the manufacturer's video drivers.

The Windows Device Driver Wizard

Windows 98 runs an "Update Device Driver Wizard" (**Figure 5.13**) when you click the Change button, which takes you through the same steps to locate new drivers on your hard drive, a CD-ROM, or in Window's complete list of display drivers.

Figure 5.13 The Windows 98 Update Device Driver Wizard lets you search for updated drivers.

3D Accelerator Cards

These days, most people who want 3D video for great gaming will simply go out and buy a 2D/3D video board to replace their old card. 3D boards include special graphics instructions in firmware designed to speed up certain kinds of graphics routines. But you can also buy 3D accelerator cards that work as additions to an installed primary display (2D) card. These cards are very cool, and if 3D matters to you at all, we recommend that you get one—unless you've already got the hottest 3D video board on the block.

Add-on 3D cards are generally available as either *daughter* cards or *pass-through* cards. A daughter card is a co-processor card that calculates data and sends it directly to the main video card for display. It is incapable of outputting a final signal to the monitor by itself, relying instead on the main video card for output. A pass-through card takes a signal from the main video card, improves it, and sends it on its way directly to the monitor.

In some cases two cards of the same type can be added to a system to provide even better 3D performance. The steps below should work for nearly all the 3D add-in cards-you're likely to find.

Installing a 3D accelerator card is one of the simplest PC upgrades. Most 3D add-in cards don't require any hardware resources, so Windows won't need to find a free interrupt or I/O address. You will, however, need a free expansion bus slot on your motherboard (most likely a PCI slot) and, of course, the manufacturer's disk/CD-ROM to install the drivers after the hardware is set up.

3D ACCELERATOR CARDS

Installing a 3D daughter card

1. Make sure your computer is turned off and open the case.

2. Locate a free expansion bus slot. All 3D add-in accelerators currently on the market are PCI bus cards, so find an empty PCI slot on your motherboard (**Figure 5.14**).

3. Remove the slot cover from the case.

4. Insert the 3D accelerator card into the slot and push it down until it is fitted correctly (**Figure 5.15**). You may need to rock it back and forth along its length to seat it properly. You should not be able to see much or any of the metal contacts that fit into the slot.

5. Attach the card's bracket to the case with the screw you removed from the slot cover (**Figure 5.16**). Note: 3D accelerator daughter cards process information and then pass it to your primary display card through the PCI bus, so no cables or wires need to be connected.

6. Leave the case open, just in case you need to return and correct any hardware problems.

Installing a 3D pass-through adapter card

1. Make sure your computer is turned off and open the case.

2. Locate a free expansion bus slot. All 3D add-in accelerators currently on the market are PCI bus cards, so you need to find an empty PCI slot on your motherboard.

3. Remove the slot cover from the case.

4. Insert the 3D accelerator card into the slot and push it down until it is correctly fitted. You may need to rock it back and forth along its length to seat it properly (**Figure 5.17**). You should not be able to

Figure 5.14 Find an empty PCI bus slot on your motherboard.

Figure 5.15 Seat the card in the slot on the motherboard.

Figure 5.16 Secure the new card with a screw to the mounting bracket.

Figure 5.17 You may need to rock the card back and forth to get it completely seated.

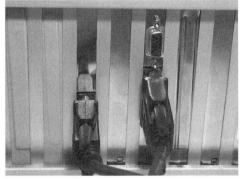

Figure 5.18 The primary video card and 3D card linked with a pass-through cable.

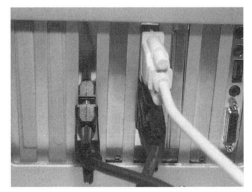

Figure 5.19 Connect your monitor to the 3D card and you're ready to go.

see much or any of the metal contacts that fit into the slot.

5. Attach the card's bracket to the case with the screw you removed from the slot cover.

6. Disconnect the monitor cable from the connector on the back of your primary video card.

7. Connect the pass-through video cable from the connector on the back of your primary video card to input connector on the new 3D accelerator card you just installed (**Figure 5.18**). The connectors on the pass-through cable allow it to be connected only one way, so you won't get confused.

8. Connect the monitor cable to the output connector on the back of the 3D add-in card, as in **Figure 5.19**.

9. As usual, you should leave the case open in case you have to correct any hardware problems.

Before you begin to install the software for your 3D add-in accelerator card, check the manufacturer's specific instructions for correct configuration. In some cases, they will contradict the steps below. For instance, the manufacturer may instruct you to ignore Windows' attempt to set up the card and use a setup program provided by the vendor. If the manufacturer's instructions contradict what we are about to tell you, ignore us and follow the manufacturer's instructions.

3D ACCELERATOR CARDS

107

Setting up 3D accelerator software

1. Turn on your computer and let Windows start.

2. Windows should detect the new hardware and tell you it's trying to determine the type of card added. Unless you have a new version of Windows 98, the operating system probably won't recognize your 3D accelerator. Windows will eventually prompt you for drivers for the new device.

3. Put the manufacturer's CD-ROM or floppy diskette into the appropriate drive and select the drive letter for the CD-ROM or floppy drive in the location dialog box (**Figure 5.20**).

4. Windows will install the drivers by copying files to the system directory. In some cases, your PC will have to reboot.

5. After Windows has restarted, it will recognize the new 3D accelerator add-in card, but the card is not necessarily ready to use yet. You may have to install additional drivers, configuration programs, and other software. Because each card is different, refer to the documentation that came with the hardware so you'll know what to do in your case.

Figure 5.20 Insert the manufacturer's CD-ROM to obtain the proper 3D drivers.

Figure 5.21 Remove the slot cover from the case.

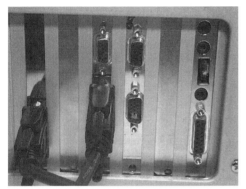

Figure 5.22 Connect the pass-through cable on the first 3D card.

Adding a Second 3D Card

Some add-on pass-through 3D accelerator cards allow you to add a second card of exactly the same type to improve performance. This is called *scan line interleaving* (SLI), a fancy term meaning that each card draws alternating lines on the screen, which speeds things up considerably. Installating the second card is similar to installing the initial card, but you should anticipate some differences in the way the cards are connected.

Second 3D pass-through card installation

1. Make sure your computer is turned off and open the case.

2. Locate a free expansion bus slot. All 3D add-in accelerators currently on the market are PCI bus cards, so find an empty PCI slot on your motherboard.

3. Remove the slot cover from the case (**Figure 5.21**).

4. Insert the 3D accelerator card into the PCI slot and push it down until it is correctly fitted. You may need to rock it back and forth along its length to seat it properly. You should not be able to see much or any of the metal contacts that fit into the slot.

5. Attach the card's bracket to the case with the screw you removed from the slot cover.

6. Connect the first pass-through cable from the video output connector on your primary video card to the video input connector on your new 3D accelerator card (**Figure 5.22**).

7. Connect the second pass-through video cable from the video output connector of the first 3D accelerator to the video input connector of the second 3D accelerator (**Figure 5.23**).

8. Connect the monitor cable to the video output connector on the back of the second 3D add-in card.

9. Leave the case open until you've configured the software and are sure everything's working properly.

✔ Tip

■ All current 3D cards that support SLI modes require that both 3D cards in the computer be of *exactly* the same type—same model, same manufacturer, same memory configuration.

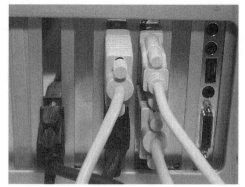

Figure 5.23 The primary video card and two 3D cards linked with pass-through cables.

AUDIO
DEVICES

6

If you only use your computer to compose
form letters in Microsoft Word, you may not
need a sound card at all—but the rest of us
do. And since most recent PCs already have
multimedia capabilities, almost everyone can
benefit from the latest advances in sound
card technology.

Whether you're an avid game player, Net
surfer, or just someone who likes to listen to
music on compact discs on your PC while
you work, you will find that many new sound
cards are chock full of great, useful features
for ridiculously low prices. Installing a new
sound card is not difficult, and we're here to
show you the way.

Installing a Sound Card

Installing a sound card is quite similar to installing the other PC cards described in this book, but a few specifics (such as instructions about the CD-ROM cable) will come in handy as you venture forth. Some sound cards require two interrupt addresses —one for use with normal Windows software, and one for use with old DOS programs. This two-address scheme may cause problems in systems that are running low on available interrupt numbers, especially since many sound boards running in DOS will only be satisfied with interrupts 5, 7, or 9.

Fortunately, DOS applications are becoming very rare these days. We say "fortunately" because often DOS programs require a number of special audio device drivers to be loaded, and they are not always installed and configured correctly by the Windows setup procedure.

We recommend that if you try to use a DOS application and it doesn't work with your new sound board, you should review the documentation that came with your sound card and visit the manufacturer's Web site for more information.

Removing an existing sound card

1. If you are replacing a sound card, turn on your computer and let Windows 95/98 start.

2. Remove the sound card from the Device Manager. Right-click the My Computer icon and select Properties from the pop-up menu. Click the Device Manager tab in the System Properties window.

3. Select your existing sound card in the device list. It should be in the "Sound, video, and game controllers" section.

4. Click the Remove button. You should also remove the joystick port device if it is a physical part of your sound card—most sound cards have a joystick port, so if you're not sure, remove it anyway. If it isn't part of your sound board, Windows will find it and reinstall support for it when you reboot.

5. When you remove hardware from your system, the Windows drivers and settings for it may remain on the system. Normally this isn't a problem, but just to be on the safe side: if an uninstall option was provided with the original sound board, go ahead and run it now.

6. The difficult part of removing a sound card is removing the DOS support—DOS device drivers and configuration settings. Unlike the Windows drivers, these DOS drivers should be deleted.

   Use Notepad or another text editor to open the file called C:\CONFIG.SYS. After you have finished editing it, you should check the C:\AUTOEXEC.BAT file.

   But before you make any changes, make a copy of these files and save them with slightly different filenames. Then read through the original files for lines that load sound card drivers. These files can be full of cryptic commands and file names, so finding the proper lines to delete sound card drivers may be difficult.

   One easy way to find the lines with sound card drivers is to look for comments. Many installation programs create these lines under a comment line, so you may have some luck finding them. Another way to find sound card drivers is to note the directory specified in the file name. If you see lines like

   DEVICE=C:\SBPRO\MCMSBP.SYS

   or

   C:\SBPRO\WAVEMIX.EXE

INSTALLING A SOUND CARD

you can assume that they are related to a Sound Blaster Pro sound card. The default location of the files is probably documented in the setup instructions that came with the sound card.

Figure 6.1 A CONFIG.SYS file displays some sound card settings.

7. Instead of deleting a line or lines in the CONFIG.SYS or AUTOEXEC.BAT files, type **REM** in front of the appropriate lines. This tells DOS that the line is a *rem*ark, and to ignore it (this is called "commenting out a line"). The advantage of commenting out a line rather than deleting it is that if you restart your computer, and see an error message, it's easy to remove the REM and enable the line again. In some cases, if you comment an important line you will have to boot from a diskette, so keep an emergency start-up diskette handy while editing these files.

If you are absolutely stumped about what to remove from the CONFIG.SYS or AUTOEXEC.BAT files, you should check the documentation for the sound card you are removing or call the manufacturer for more information.

8. There are two more files to check for old sound board settings before you move on. They are the WIN.INI and SYSTEM.INI files, and you'll find them in the \WINDOWS directory. Once again, back up these files before making any changes to them.

These files may have some sound card settings in them. Chances are the settings will be grouped under a heading that relates to your sound card. (But no guarantees!)

To comment-out a line in the WIN.INI or SYSTEM.INI file, put a semi-colon at the start of the line. Again, you should refer to your documentation if you have

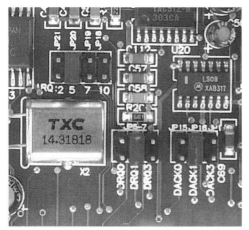

Figure 6.2 The jumpers on a sound card control the IRQ setting.

Figure 6.3 The MIDI port on most sound cards doubles as a joystick port.

any questions about what to remove from your WIN.INI or SYSTEM.INI files.

9. After you have checked these files, shut down your PC, unplug it, and physically remove the sound card from the system.

10. Start your computer again to confirm that the system starts without any sound card errors. If you see error messages during startup, re-check your CONFIG.SYS, AUTOEXEC.BAT, WIN.INI, and SYSTEM.INI files.

11. Click the System icon (in the Control Panel) and go into the Device Manager to make sure the old sound board is no longer listed. If it is gone, turn off the PC, unplug it, and proceed with installing the new sound board.

As with any new adapter card, Plug and Play or PCI sound cards should configure themselves correctly when the system is booted. If you have a problem during the installation, see the section "When Plug and Play won't work" in Chapter 2.

Sound card pre-installation

In the unlikely case that you are installing a non-Plug N Play ISA sound card, or are not using a Plug N Play operating system like Windows 95/98, you must select an interrupt for the card before putting it into the PC. Sound cards generally use IRQ 5, which works fine unless you happen to have two printer ports—LPT2 also uses IRQ 5.

The IRQ setting is usually controlled by one (or sometimes more than one) jumper (**Figure 6.2**) on the sound card, or by a setup utility provided on the manufacturer's CD-ROM or diskette. Check the sound card's documentation or look for labeling printed on the card itself near any jumpers you find.

Most sound cards include a MIDI port that doubles as a joystick port (**Figure 6.3**). If you intend to use the joystick port on your sound card, make sure that you do not have another joystick port enabled in your system. This is rarely an issue; most PC joystick ports are part of a sound card.

Sound card installation

1. Make sure your PC is unplugged.

2. Find an empty expansion slot that matches your sound card and remove the cover that corresponds to this slot from the back of the computer case.

3. Insert the new sound card into the empty slot. You may have to push it down with some force to make sure it is seated correctly (**Figure 6.4**)—the metal contacts that fit into the slot should be almost completely hidden. If the card is reluctant to slip down completely, you can rock it back and forth to fit one end, then the other.

4. Fasten the new sound card to the computer case with a screw.

5. Attach speakers, microphones, earphones, or any other input/output devices you want to connect to the back of the board. Make sure you are using the right jacks; check the documentation if you're not sure (**Figure 6.5**).

    If you are connecting *unpowered* speakers (meaning you don't have to plug them into the wall), they should plug into the mini-stereo port labeled Speaker. The Line Out port is meant to connect to an external amplifier and does not provide sufficient amplification for unpowered speakers. In fact, even powered speakers will be happier on the Speaker connector.

    Be very careful not to connect anything to the microphone port except a microphone. Connecting *any* other device (such as the output from a CD player) can over-drive this connection and damage your sound card.

Figure 6.4 A sound card will slip into a PCI slot like the ones shown.

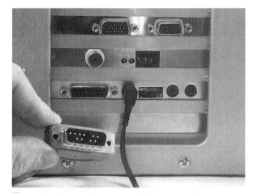

Figure 6.5 A sound card usually has several connectors.

INSTALLING A SOUND CARD

6. Leave the PC's cover off while you install the drivers and configure your new hardware. If you need to make changes, you'll save some time by not having to take it off again.

Sound card features

The newest trend in computer sound hardware is three-dimensional (3-D) audio reproduction. This usually involves at least four speakers connected to the sound card and creates a sound environment in which sound effects and music seem to come from any direction. This can make computer games totally thrilling. Competing software standards are generally well supported by all new sound cards, so you can probably use one sound card with all 3-D audio-enabled games. Not all 3-D sound is equal, so you should test your potential sound board in the store before you buy.

New sound cards are all PCI bus adapter cards. PCI adapter cards improve the overall performance of a computer because the faster bus speed allows the CPU to spend less time talking to the sound card and more time running the program.

Historically, the de facto standard for sound hardware is Creative Labs' Sound Blaster. The Sound Blaster standard is still important for PC operating systems such as DOS or Linux. If you run DOS or Linux software or games, make sure your new sound board supports Sound Blaster emulation.

Many low-cost sound cards produce synthesized music with an inexpensive FM-synthesis chip that may sound "electronic" and phony. High-end sound cards use a more advanced technique called *wave-table synthesis*. With this technique, the sound from actual musical instruments is sampled and used to play the notes in the song, making for a more realistic musical track.

The number of MIDI *voices* that a sound card can produce affects the quality of its synthesized music. A sound card that can produce only 16 sounds at the same time cannot keep up with the ambience produced by a 32, 64, or 128-voice sound card. Of course, you pay more for more simultaneous voices, but it makes synthesized music sound much better. You should realize, though, that the number of voices only affects the quality of synthesized MIDI music, not most computer game sound effects, WAV files, or CD audio.

In addition to stereo output and 3D audio output, it is now possible to get sound cards that support the new digital surround sound standards. If you are planning to watch DVD movies on your computer, or play games that support digital surround sound, then you should check out these sound cards.

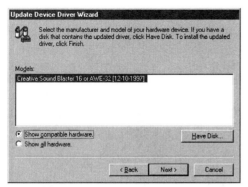

Figure 6.6 If Windows does not have the right driver, you'll need to use the disk that came with the card.

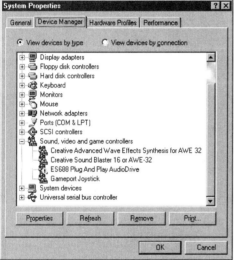

Figure 6.7 The Device Manager shows you any problem devices. Note the warning sign beside the hardware device.

Sound Card Configuration

Configuring your sound card in the Windows environment should be fairly painless. However, as with all PC-related activities, something can go wrong during installation, not work right afterward, or just annoy you. This section takes you through the steps for configuring your sound card software for Windows 95/98 and Windows NT and can help you avoid difficulties.

Configuring sound card software

1. Turn on your PC and let Windows start.

   Windows should detect your new sound card and prompt you to load a driver from its driver list or the manufacturer's CD-ROM or diskette. In some cases, Windows may detect the wrong type of sound card. If Windows tries to install the wrong drivers, or if the installation fails, you should remove the sound card and associated files and start over. See the section "Removing an existing sound card" earlier in this chapter.

2. When you see the "Found New Hardware" message and are prompted for drivers, click on the Have Disk... button and insert the disk or CD-ROM provided by the manufacturer (**Figure 6.6**).

3. Windows will copy files to the hard drive and continue loading.

4. If Windows did not detect your new sound card while booting, look in the Device Manager to see if any problem devices are shown (**Figure 6.7**). Right-click on My Computer on the desktop and select Properties. Click the Device Manager tab and check for any devices marked by a yellow warning icon. If your sound card is not shown, go to step 6 to run the Add New Hardware Wizard.

5. If your sound card or any other device appears with a yellow warning icon, double-click the errant device and read the device status message. If you have a hardware resource problem such as an interrupt conflict, then you should see the section "When Plug N Play won't work" in Chapter 2 to resolve the hardware resource issues causing the problem. If there doesn't seem to be a hardware resource problem, then you should check for an installation program on the CD-ROM or diskette provided by the manufacturer. In some cases, Windows cannot load the proper drivers and configuration settings when it detects the new sound card—the manufacturer's setup program must be run. Check the documentation that came with the sound card for more information.

6. To run the Add New Hardware Wizard, open the Control Panel and double-click the Add New Hardware icon. Follow the prompts and allow Windows to search for new hardware (**Figure 6.9**). Windows will attempt to find drivers for the new hardware. You may be prompted for a location for these drivers, so have your disk or CD-ROM handy.

7. If Windows fails to detect your new hardware at startup and in the Add New Hardware Wizard, then you should check that your sound card is properly seated in its slot. If it appears to be inserted correctly, run through the steps in the section "Removing an existing sound card" earlier in this chapter to make sure that there are no leftover files or configuration settings from an earlier installation. Finally, check the sound card documentation or contact the manufacturer if you cannot resolve the problem yourself.

Figure 6.8 You can manually override the IRQ settings to reveal the conflict.

Figure 6.9 Use the Add New Hardware Wizard to set up your card.

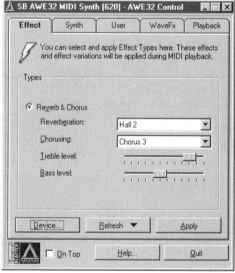

Figure 6.10 Be sure to load the utilities provided by the sound card manufacturer to get the most out of your card.

SOUND CARD CONFIGURATION

Figure 6.11 Click on the Multimedia Icon.

Figure 6.12 Click on the Windows NT Multimedia Devices tab.

8. After successfully adding your new sound card, install the programs and utilities provided by the manufacturer to make sure you get the best performance and compatibility for games and other multimedia applications (**Figure 6.10**).

Most sound cards come with utilities that showcase the features of the hardware. These utilities may allow you to create, edit, and store digital sound files. If your sound card features wave-table synthesis, you can load different instruments and effects into the card to experiment with music effects. Sound cards that support 3D audio or digital surround sound almost always come with neat demos that show off this feature.

Windows NT does not automatically detect new hardware, so you have to manually add drivers for your sound card. Follow these steps:

Configuring sound cards in Windows NT

1. Open the Control Panel in Windows NT and double-click the Multimedia icon (**Figure 6.11**).

2. Click on the last tab, Multimedia Devices, and confirm that no device matches the sound card you have installed, as in **Figure 6.12**.

3. Click the Add button and check the list of supported devices for the sound card you want to add (**Figure 6.13**). If you do not see it, select "Other or Unlisted Device" and point to the directory or disk where the manufacturer's drivers are located.

4. After Windows NT copies files to the hard drive, it will prompt you to reboot. The sound card should work normally when the system restarts.

✔ Tip

- Adding a sound card to your system may cause an error in another device that tries to use the same IRQ or I/O address. Even though the sound card is not the first device to use the address, it can supersede an existing hardware component. See the section "Correcting installation problems" in Chapter 2.

Windows 3.1 issues

As mentioned in previous chapters, Windows 3.1 does not auto-detect new hardware. In order to configure the sound card drivers under Windows 3.1 you must know the hardware resources that your new audio device is using. Open the Control Panel and double-click the Drivers icon. You must select a driver from the rather short list of provided drivers or click the Have Disk... button to load them from the manufacturer's CD-ROM or diskette. Keep the Windows 3.1 installation diskettes handy because Windows will need them to load multimedia support.

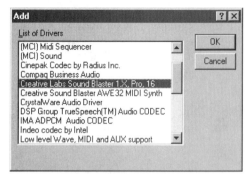

Figure 6.13 Click on the Add button to see if Windows contains the drivers for your card.

Figure 6.14 A USB plug (from USB speakers) ready for connection into the USB port.

SOUND CARD CONFIGURATION

USB Speakers

If the thought of installing a sound card makes you uncomfortable, even after reading through this chapter, then there is an easy alternative that will work with most new PCs. If your computer features a Universal Serial Bus (USB) connector, then you can plug USB speakers directly into the USB port. Since USB speakers do not require a sound card, you don't even have to turn off your PC, much less open the case.

Though USB speakers have some drawbacks, which we will discuss later, they do have one important advantage: Plug them in, and Windows 98 makes them work.

✔ Tip

- USB devices work great with Windows 98, and some recent revisions of Windows 95, but if you bought your Windows 95 PC before 1998 you may have to upgrade to Windows 98 in order to use USB speakers.

Installing USB speakers

1. The USB speaker hardware is very easy to install: Plug the speakers into the USB port. Windows 98 will detect the new speakers and prompt you to install drivers from the manufacturer when you plug them in. That's it. This is probably the most significant advantage that you will realize from these speaker systems.

2. Since USB speaker systems share the universal serial bus with other devices, they may interfere with the sound hardware. A USB scanner, modem, or joystick (for example) may be sending a large amount of data through the USB port and blocking the sound information to your USB speakers. Unfortunately, the only remedy is to stop using the other USB devices when you want your speakers to work without interruption.

USB SPEAKERS

3. The signal supplied to the speakers is purely digital, so the sound reproduction is supposed to be crystal clear, though you may be hard pressed to tell the difference between high-end speakers plugged into a high-end sound card and high-end USB speakers.

✔ Tips

■ Since USB sound systems do not have dedicated hardware to process sound signals, they use more CPU power to make noise. This means that USB speakers are not the optimum sound hardware for games, though most multimedia and business applications are not as processor-intensive and are served well by USB speaker systems.

■ If you use your computer strictly for business applications, listening to audio CDs, and surfing the Internet, then USB speakers are a very simple way to add audio capabilities to your system. However, if you depend on your sound hardware for reliable output under all circumstances, play computer games, or already have a number of USB devices connected, then you should seriously consider avoiding USB sound hardware.

USB SPEAKERS

MEMORY, CPUS, AND MOTHERBOARDS

7

In this chapter, we deal with the three upgrades that can make the most significant improvement to your system. The three components whose upgrades we explore are memory, CPUs (central processing units or *processors*), and motherboards. To improve the raw performance of your PC, you'll have to look into changing one, two, or all three of these things.

The processor, or CPU, is the brain of your computer, so putting a more powerful CPU into your machine boosts performance too. But this is not always possible, so you'll have to consider many things before you begin. In some situations you might decide to upgrade the motherboard in order to install a new class of processor.

The motherboard is the ultimate challenge when it comes to PC upgrading—in fact, in many cases a motherboard transplant is a bad idea. Not because it is terribly complicated in and of itself but because removing the motherboard disrupts every other part of your PC, and may not be cost effective compared to buying a new PC. Not to worry, though—this chapter walks you through the decision tree, and if you decide to go ahead we'll show you how to proceed.

Upgrading Memory

Lots of memory (or RAM) is essential for running graphic user interfaces such as Windows 95, 98 and NT, not to mention most contemporary software programs. Fortunately, memory is one of the easiest things to upgrade in your PC.

Adding more memory can be the single most cost-effective way to improve the performance of your PC. Systems with too little RAM must use the hard drive to store information temporarily (known as *swapping*), and because the fastest hard drive is still many times slower than RAM, the more information that must be swapped to the hard disk, the slower the system will run.

A few years ago, new computers came with only 4 or 8 MB of RAM—far too little for today's applications. 16MB is now considered the bare minimum for Windows 95/98, and 32MB or even 64MB is not too much. In some cases, adding memory will allow you to achieve performance several times better than you have now. Even with only a 25 to 50-percent improvement in performance, it is still a worthwhile upgrade. The price of RAM has also come down sharply in recent years.

There are two considerations to make before running out to purchase more RAM for your computer. First, you have to know the kind of RAM modules you need. Second, you need to know how many RAM modules will fit into your motherboard. Check out the section "The background on memory" for more information.

Figure 7.1 The RAM on your motherboard is fairly easy to spot. Unused RAM slots are often nearby.

Installing RAM

1. Make sure your computer is unplugged.

2. Open the computer case and find the memory banks (RAM slots) on your motherboard (**Figure 7.1**).

   In some cases the RAM is hidden under other components—you may have to

Figure 7.2 If there are no free RAM slots, you'll have to remove an existing memory module.

Figure 7.3 Many types of RAM clip in to their slots.

remove hard drives, adapter cards, or even the power supply to get to it.

3. If you have no free RAM slots and need more memory, you must remove the existing low-capacity memory modules to make room for new higher-capacity memory modules (**Figure 7.2**).

4. Add the new memory modules to the RAM slots.

SIMMs slip into the slot at a 45-degree angle, and then snap into alignment as you tilt them into a vertical position and the clips at both ends of the slot grab them (**Figure 7.3**). DIMMs can be pushed straight into their slots. See the section "The background on memory" for more about SIMMS, DIMMs, and other types of memory.

5. After the memory is installed and appears to be seated properly, you're ready to turn on your computer. As always, reconnect any cables you had to disconnect, but leave the case cover off until you have confirmed the new hardware is functioning correctly.

Getting your PC to recognize a new memory configuration is very easy. In most cases you just turn on the computer and let it detect the memory.

However, with some older systems you may need to follow these additional steps.

Configuring your new RAM

1. If your computer beeps more than once or shows a screen message saying that the memory size is wrong, go into the BIOS setup routine and let the computer save the new memory configuration. See the section "BIOS" in Chapter 2 for more on changing BIOS options.

In most computers, you are prompted to enter the Setup menu automatically when the memory size causes an error (**Figure 7.4**). If this is not the case, just reboot the machine and start the Setup menu as you normally would—by pressing Del as the machine starts up.

2. In the Setup menu, find the screen that displays the total RAM in the system (**Figure 7.5**).

   This is never an editable field—the system should detect the amount of memory installed. However, if the total shown does not agree with how much RAM you already had plus the amount of RAM you installed, then one of four things is wrong: Your memory modules are installed incorrectly, the memory is bad, you have used the wrong memory banks, or you have installed the wrong kind of memory.

3. Once you have found the memory total displayed in the BIOS and confirmed the amount is correct, simply exit the BIOS Setup menu normally, making sure you save changes.

Your computer should restart and boot normally. In Windows 95/98, you can confirm the amount of memory that the operating system detects by right-clicking the My Computer icon and selecting Properties (**Figure 7.6**).

The background on memory

The first PCs used memory chips called DRAM (Dynamic Random Access Memory). PCs that use this memory type today are rare. After DRAMs came SIMMs (Single Inline Memory Modules). A SIMM is a small, printed circuit board with RAM chips attached to one or both sides. The SIMMs either connect directly to your motherboard or to a memory board that fits into a special slot. SIMMs commonly come in 30-pin or 72-pin form. Because the physical size of these two types is similar, you must take note of the number of pins on the module—or observe that 72-

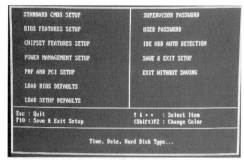

Figure 7.4 If your newly installed memory is causing a problem, you'll get bounced into the BIOS menu.

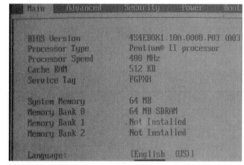

Figure 7.5 This is the "total RAM installed" screen in a typical BIOS.

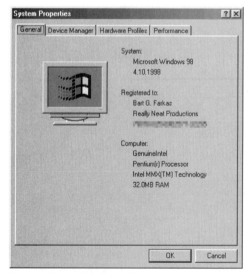

Figure 7.6 You can get the skinny on your system's memory by right-clicking on the My Computer icon and selecting Properties.

pin SIMMs have a notch dividing the metal connectors in half. Most 386 and many 486 PCs require 30-pin SIMMs, though some 486s also accept 72-pin SIMMs.

In the last few years, RAM modules have changed to a DIMM (Dual Inline Memory Module) form factor. DIMMs are longer than SIMMs and usually wider, and advances in chip manufacturing make the DIMM modules noticeably thinner than the older SIMM modules. DIMMs slide into a slot straight-on and are clipped into place with small levers at each end. There is an off-center notch along the contact edge so that there is only one way to insert the module correctly.

Different motherboards support different memory module formats, and some motherboards will even support different formats at the same time. Check the documentation that came with your computer or motherboard for this information. The documentation should also tell you how many memory modules you can install in your system, though you can determine that yourself by opening the computer case and counting the memory slots

All PC memory comes with a speed rating that refers to how quickly data can be accessed. Common speed ratings for SIMMs fall between 60 to 90 nanoseconds. The lower numbers mean shorter access times and better performance—and higher prices.

Starting with the Pentium processor, SIMMs that supported *extended data-out* functions (EDO) could be used. EDO memory was the preferred format for Pentium systems until DIMMs became available. DIMM speed was originally rated like SIMMs, but recently has been rated for the bus speed with which it is warranted to operate. The newest Pentium III processor systems require PC100 compliant SDRAM—meaning that the memory is rated to work in systems with a 100 MHz front-side bus.

What kind of memory should you buy?

Obviously, your new memory must be the same kind as the memory already in your computer. It's OK to buy memory rated faster than what you've already got; it's not OK to buy memory that's rated slower. If you're not sure what's in there now, remove one of the modules and take it with you to the computer store, or have it ready when you order your new memory over the phone. Your motherboard or computer system documentation will also probably list the speed and kind of memory you need. There are also Web sites called configurators that will tell you what kind of memory your computer needs—you just select your model. Search Yahoo for "memory configurator." If you cannot determine the memory speed by any of these methods, call your computer vendor and ask.

SIMM and DIMM removal

To remove a SIMM, spread the end brackets and gently tilt the SIMM down to about a 45-degree angle. Then slide it out. You have to remove SIMMs in order—start with the one that has room to lean away from the others first. DIMM modules pop out of their slots by flipping the fastener lever at both ends of the slot. The module should come straight out.

Pairing up SIMMs

Pentium systems require SIMMs to be installed in pairs, but 486 systems accept single modules. However, some 486 systems do not recognize the full capacity of a SIMM if it has memory chips soldered to both sides of the memory module. If you boot the system and find it recognizes only half of the memory, you must replace the SIMMs with 486-compatible modules.

Error Checking and Correcting RAM

Some high-end PC workstations and file servers use a special type of memory called ECC (Error Checking and Correcting) RAM, which is able to detect and correct memory errors. The frequency of memory errors is quite low, so most people are not willing to pay the premium price for ECC. Some SIMMs can detect memory errors by storing a *parity bit*. This type of memory is not as good as ECC RAM at checking and correcting errors, but it was common for a while because it was only marginally more expensive than non-parity memory. You cannot mix parity and non-parity memory modules in a PC.

Memory banks and slots

Memory *slots* are often referred to as memory *banks* in your motherboard documentation, and are numbered starting from zero. These banks must be populated in a specific order, usually from lowest to highest. If you have misplaced the documentation for your motherboard, you may be able to find the correct arrangement through trial and error. If you are populating all the memory banks in your system you won't have to worry about this.

✔ Tip

- Be sure to populate the memory banks of Pentium systems with pairs of SIMMs of exactly the same capacity and speed.

Upgrading the CPU

If your motherboard and Central Processing Unit (CPU) are both designed to allow you to upgrade the CPU, then you're in luck—because this is one of the simplest procedures to do inside a PC.

In general, you can only upgrade to a faster version of the same class of CPU that you currently have. That is, if you've got a 486 now, you might be able to install a faster 486—but you can't just drop in a Pentium II. Upgrading the CPU can give you a noticeable improvement in performance, especially if you're moving from the slowest to the fastest CPU in any family. There is a class of CPUs made specifically for upgrading PCs. These are called *overdrive CPUs*. With an overdrive CPU, you may be able to achieve Pentium-class performance in a system that originally housed a 486 CPU.

Preparing to upgrade your CPU

Check your motherboard documentation (**Figure 7.7**) and confirm that the upgrade CPU you want to put into your computer is supported by your motherboard. If your system documentation doesn't provide this information, call your PC vendor and ask.

For example, the Intel Pentium processor: Newer Pentiums use a lower voltage than the early ones did. As a result, you usually can't drop a newer, faster Pentium into your older Pentium motherboard. But there are exceptions, so call your vendor. Also look at the CPU Upgrade Table later in this chapter.

Also, some motherboards support processors from different manufacturers. First, though, you must confirm that the CPU you want to run is compatible with the motherboard you have. This is not a trivial matter.

CPU speed is not controlled by the CPU itself, as you might expect, but by the moth-

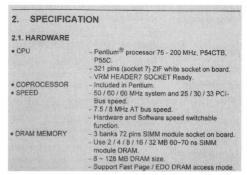

Figure 7.7 Your motherboard documentation will tell you which CPUs your motherboard can support.

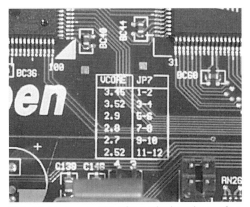

Figure 7.8 Jumper settings for motherboards are often printed on the motherboard itself.

erboard. Two factors determine the CPU speed: the speed of the system bus and the multiplication factor of the processor. Most motherboards require that you set the bus speed and the CPU multiplier factor with jumpers, though some motherboards let you set this and other factors in the BIOS setup menus.

The motherboard documentation will note the proper bus speed and CPU multiplier for the CPU you want to install. If you cannot find the documentation, look at the motherboard itself—the jumper settings are often explained in a chart printed on the surface of the board. Or call your system vendor.

Newer versions of the same processor family may use a different CPU voltage. Some motherboards automatically sense the processor and select the right voltage, others require you to select the voltage with jumpers, and some won't support a different voltage at all. The motherboard documentation should tell you how (and whether) you can change the voltage to the CPU (**Figure 7.8**).

✔ Tip

■ The information about CPU upgrades in this chapter is for desktop PCs and is not applicable to laptop PCs. Laptops are not normally meant to be upgraded by users. Refer to your vendor for more information on upgrade possibilities.

See also Appendix B for a very large table that can help you determine your CPU upgrade options.

You will notice that the overdrive processors can upgrade some slower CPUs to a level that exceeds the upgrade for a faster CPU. This is because the overdrive CPU speed depends on the system bus speed and the clock multiplier in the overdrive CPU. For example: A Pentium 90 processor on a socket 5 motherboard uses a bus speed of 60 MHz and can be upgraded with an overdrive CPU that has a

UPGRADING THE CPU

clock multiplier of 3 to 180 MHz. A Pentium 133 processor on a socket 5 motherboard uses a bus speed of 66 MHz and can be upgraded with an overdrive CPU that has a clock multiplier of 2.5 to 166 MHz.

Does this mean that the Pentium 133 system is less upgradeable than the Pentium 90 system? No. The overdrive upgrade guidelines assume that you do not change the settings of your motherboard before upgrading. If you adjust the system bus speed before upgrading, you can pick the bus speed that allows you to install the fastest upgrade processor possible.

Upgrading your CPU

1. Unplug your computer and remove the cover, as in **Figure 7.9**.

2. Locate the CPU and remove it, as shown in **Figure 7.10**.

   In most cases, the CPU is on the motherboard. All CPUs before the Pentium II are mounted on a socket. Pentium IIs, some Celerons, and some Pentium IIIs use a CPU package that mounts into a slot, imaginatively called *slot 1*.

   You may have to remove the system power supply in order to get clear access to the CPU.

   One word of warning: If you have to remove the power supply, be very careful not to open it. Inside, capacitors and other components store and conduct electricity and they can be accidentally discharged quite easily. The power supply is normally attached to the case by four screws that are accessible on the back, outside of the case. Only these four screws should be removed.

3. Remove ZIF (Zero Insertion Force) socket CPUs by flipping the locking mechanism arm up (**Figure 7.11**). ZIF sockets lock and unlock the CPU with a lever attached to the side of the socket.

Figure 7.9 Remove the cover from your PC.

Figure 7.10 Locate the CPU.

Figure 7.11 Socketed CPUs often have a flipping arm that acts as a locking mechanism.

Figure 7.12 Slot 1 CPUs can be removed by flipping the clips at each end of the processor.

	486DX /DX2	486SX PGA	487SX /DX3T
JP15	1-2	2-3	1-2
JP16	Short	Open	Short
JP18	2-3	Open	1-2
JP20	1-2	1-2	2-3

CACHE SIZE (BYTE)	ALT SEL JP23, JP24		TAG SEL JP26, JP27	
128K	1-	1-2	1-2	2-3
256K	2-3	1-2	1-2	1-2

Banks		
Type	1	2
Jump	21 22 25	21 22 25
32K X 8	1-2 1-2 1-2	2-3 2-3 1-2
	Total 128K	Total 256K

Figure 7.13 Adjust the jumpers on your motherboard.

The CPU should pull free without resistance. But it may not; all those pins can produce a lot of friction. Make sure you have pushed the ZIF lever all the way up. Some CPU heat sinks are clipped to the socket with metal or plastic tabs and must be released before the CPU can be extracted. On the other hand, some heat sinks and heat sink fans are glued directly to the CPU and can be removed as one piece with the processor.

Slot 1 CPUs can be removed by flipping the clips at each end of the processor package, as in **Figure 7.12**. The package can then be pulled free. You'll feel some resistance, so you may have to rock the package back and forth along its length. In some systems, the heat sink is also fastened to the CPU package and the motherboard and must be unclipped from one or both before the package can be extracted.

If you do not have a ZIF socket, then you will have to pry the CPU out of its socket. This procedure will require a chip-extractor tool (see Chapter 1 for more on tools). be very careful—don't bend or break any of the CPU pins while working it free.

4. This is the best time to change the required jumpers on the motherboard (**Figure 7.13**). Follow the documentation that came with your system or motherboard.

   Usually, you are required to set the CPU voltage, system bus speed, and CPU multiplier. On 486 systems, you'll have no choice about CPU voltage so you can skip this setting. Before moving any jumpers, always write down the original positions, or better yet, take a photo.

   If you do not have the motherboard documentation handy, you may find the jumpers explained by markings on the motherboard. These charts are not always printed near the jumpers that you need to change, but might be printed on any clear area of the board. You may have to look carefully to find them.

5. Carefully fit the new CPU into the socket or slot (**Figure 7.14**), being sure not to bend any of the pins. Line up pins with socket holes very cautiously.

Note that in socket systems the CPU is oriented only one way—one corner of the CPU and socket has a pin missing (**Figure 7.15**). These corners must be lined up. The CPU should drop effortlessly into the socket. If it does not, then the socket is not fully opened, the CPU is not aligned, or some of the CPU pins are bent. When the processor is correctly seated, slide the locking arm down to lock it in place.

Slot 1 processor packages fit into their slots much like adapter cards fit into expansion ports. There is a gap in the edge of the processor package where the metal connector tabs line up. This gap can only fit into the slot one way, so make sure it's lined up with the gap in the slot, as in **Figure 7.16**. Push the package all the way down until it stops moving to ensure a perfect connection. The release clips should click to lock the processor into place.

In non-ZIF sockets you have to press the CPU down until it is fully inserted into the socket. Try to push it down evenly and don't push too quickly or you could damage the motherboard if it flexes too much.

6. You should be able to reuse the heat sink from the processor you just removed if the new CPU does not include one.

Most CPUs faster than a 486 will have a heat sink or a fan for heat dissipation (see **Figure 7.17**). The heat sink should be attached to the CPU with heat sink resin or glue. If the heat sink was glued onto

Figure 7.14 Fit the new CPU into the socket (shown here) or slot.

Figure 7.15 Note the missing pin on the upper right corner of this socket CPU. This will help you know how to line up the CPU with the processor socket on the motherboard.

Figure 7.16 Place the slot 1 CPU into the slot. The connector tabs fit in only one way.

Figure 7.17 This is a typical heat sink for a socket CPU.

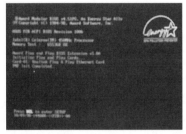

Figure 7.18 The BIOS POST screen identifies your CPU speed after you've installed the new CPU.

the original CPU with heat resin, add a little more to ensure good conduction of heat away from the new CPU (you can buy resin at some computer stores). If the processor heat sink also includes a fan, make sure that the power lead is connected so the fan will spin.

You are ready to turn on the system and try out the new CPU.

7. You should probably leave the case cover off while testing, since you may find jumper settings that are incorrect or that the heat sink fan is not properly connected.

8. When you turn on the computer, watch for the BIOS POST screen to indicate the correct CPU speed (**Figure 7.18**). If it does not show the correct CPU speed, then you should turn off the computer immediately and recheck all the jumpers that control the CPU speed.

You will not damage your system if you turn it off during the POST, but you could do some damage if you let it run at a clock speed that is too high. Running at a clock speed that is lower than you expected is not harmful, but you won't be getting the full benefit from your new processor.

Also watch for the indicated CPU voltage on the POST screen. If it does not match the CPU that you have installed, turn off your computer immediately! If you run the processor at a voltage that is too high it will cause damage to the CPU and the motherboard very quickly. Re-check the voltage setting jumpers and confirm the correct voltage for your new CPU.

Burning in

Many hardware technicians recommend that you *burn-in* new components for a long period of time—suggestions range from 8 to 48 hours. Though it is a good idea to test all of your new hardware this way, it is perhaps most crucial for CPUs. Processor problems will most likely show up within a day. Your system should be stable while running 24 hours a day, seven days a week, so a one-day burn-in should pose no problems.

To burn-in your CPU, re-assemble the case cover and leave your computer turned on for 24 to 48 hours. Disable any power-saving features that slow down the processor or put the computer into a sleep mode. Look for the Power Management icon in the Windows Control Panel to find and disable these power-saving settings. You do not have to run an application during the burn-in period—just let your screen-saver kick in.

Check the machine at short intervals for the first few hours. Put your hand over the fan exhaust on the power supply at the back of the case to check the temperature of the airflow. It will probably feel warm, but if it is hot, you smell anything abnormal (like burning insulation), or the power supply fan is not running, shut down the computer and let it cool for ten minutes before rebooting. With the cover off, confirm that the CPU and power supply fans are working. If your system runs consistently hot, you should consider adding another fan to the front of the case to draw air into the system.

CPU and bus speeds

A 100 MHz CPU may be running on a system bus clocked at 33 MHz and a CPU multiplier of 3. Because 33 times 3 equals 99, the CPU is considered to be running at 100 MHz. (Actually, the system bus is usually 33.3 MHz, making the CPU run at 99.9 MHz.) Another 100 MHz CPU may be running on a system bus clocked at 50 MHz and a CPU multiplier of 2. The CPU performance is the same in both cases, but the higher bus speed of the second system results in better disk and memory performance. Unfortunately, this higher bus speed may not be stable for all components of the system (RAM is notoriously sensitive to clock speed), so the system with the 33 MHz bus speed might be more stable. If you have problems with instability, try a different combination of bus speed and multiplier settings.

Overclocking your processor

Overclocking refers to setting the bus speed and CPU multiplier to run the CPU faster than its rated speed. Though it voids your system warranty (not just the CPU warranty—the warranty of every component in the system), overclocking has become a popular way of getting extra performance from a PC without spending extra money, and tests show that most of the time it does no harm.

But take care: Besides losing warranty support, overclocking carries other risks. Overclocking the CPU creates more heat than it is rated to withstand. Obviously, this can be a dangerous situation, so you might want to protect your overclocked system by installing extra CPU cooling features like an extra fan, or even a liquid-cooling system.

In general it's a bad idea to overclock a brand-new system that cost you a fortune, but doing so to an older system to extend its usefulness a little further may be worth it. In most cases, you can only overclock a system by one or two steps—for example, a 100 MHz CPU can be overclocked to 120 or 133 MHz. Doubling the speed of a CPU and still having a stable system is highly unlikely.

Symptoms of an unstable overclocked system can range from boot failures and system crashes to smoke and flames pouring out of the case. Before you take the plunge, do some research—you'll find plenty of information about overclocking on the Internet. Or you could even ask a friendly tech on your system vendor's support line.

UPGRADING THE CPU

Heat Sinks

Heat sinks are special radiators that sit on your processor and help dissipate the heat produced by the processor. Heat sink resin (or glue) ensures proper contact and heat conduction from the ceramic processor casing to the heat sink. The processor will get hotter if you skip the resin. If your system is running hot already, lack of resin may push it into an unstable zone.

Upgrading the Motherboard

Changing the motherboard in a PC is easier than it used to be, but it's still a very long and involved process. Nearly every component must be removed to gain access, and usually key components like memory and video boards must be upgraded to maintain compatibility with the new board. For this reason, upgrading a system motherboard can cost you more than you might expect—especially if you don't consider the compatibility of core components beforehand. Ironically, the motherboard itself is one of the least expensive items in the whole system.

Before you upgrade

A motherboard upgrade is usually required when you want to install a new generation of CPU. Otherwise, there's not much reason to upgrade, especially when you consider the time and expense involved.

You should be able to use most of your existing hardware with your new motherboard: disk drives, CD-ROM and DVD-ROM drives, modems, keyboards, the mouse, printers, and most adapter cards. The exceptions to this are listed in the "Motherboard compatibility" section later in this chapter.

There are a few common computer case/motherboard sizes or formats. The earliest PCs used XT format motherboards. Then the AT format became the standard. Once the Pentium II processors came along, the ATX format gained popularity.

Some computer cases do not fit any standard format motherboards. Many of the big name PC manufacturers design and build their own proprietary format motherboards and cases with odd dimensions. Surprisingly, generic-brand PCs tend to have the most compatible computer cases. You will save a little money if you can reuse your case.

The Pentium II processors are mainly found on ATX format motherboards. These require ATX cases with an ATX power supply. An AT-format motherboard will not fit correctly into an ATX case and vice versa, and the power connectors from the power supply to the motherboard are incompatible between the AT and ATX formats. You may be able to find AT format motherboards for Pentium II CPUs that allow you to use your AT case, but you'll miss some of the advanced energy features of the newer format.

✔ Tip

■ If you find that replacing your motherboard means you also have to replace the RAM, video card, and case, then consider simply buying a whole new PC—an appealing plan given the amazingly low prices new systems go for today, not to mention the three-year warranty.

Due to the complexity and time it takes to replace a motherboard, this procedure should only be attempted by those who have experience working with PC hardware. For most users, avoiding it is worth the cost of buying a new system, or having the motherboard replaced by a PC technician. We provide the following procedure only for those courageous readers who are eager to learn more about computer hardware.

Removing the old board

1. Be forewarned: This procedure takes a long time. Expert PC techies can do it in less than an hour, but if this is your first motherboard transplant, you should budget at least four hours. Fortunately, you do not have to complete the procedure all at once—if you have the space to leave your computer's guts lying around, you can attack the job in pieces.

UPGRADING THE MOTHERBOARD

2. Back up the information on your hard drive (**Figure 7.19**), and then verify the backup.

Replacing a motherboard is a major upgrade and the potential for disaster is much higher than the other procedures described in this book. If you ever back up your system, this is the time to do it!

3. Go into the BIOS setup screens in your system and write down the settings of every item on every screen in the BIOS. If you have problems with the new motherboard BIOS setup, referring to the old configuration can be a huge help. Also see Chapter 2 for more on the BIOS.

4. Turn off your computer, unplug it, and remove the cover.

This is a good time to verify that the components you intend to use with your new motherboard are compatible (see **Figure 7.20**). Check the RAM modules, video card, and other adapter cards you're using now to confirm that they will fit into the correct places on your new motherboard and eyeball the new motherboard to make sure it will fit correctly into the case. Ignoring this checkpoint can be frustrating if you find that you must buy new components after your computer is disassembled. You will have no system to use while you wait for your needed hardware.

5. Unplug all the connectors attached to your PC if you have not already done so (**Figure 7.21**). If you have a Polaroid camera, take pictures of the back of the case so that you can refer to it if you have problems re-connecting external items. Sticky-notes are a great help in labeling the connectors.

6. Remove all the adapter cards plugged into your motherboard (**Figure 7.22**) including their connecting cables. Again, take pictures of the inside of your case

Figure 7.19 Back up your hard drive.

Figure 7.20 Check to see that the cards you currently own will fit into your new motherboard.

Figure 7.21 Unplug the connectors attached to your PC.

UPGRADING THE MOTHERBOARD

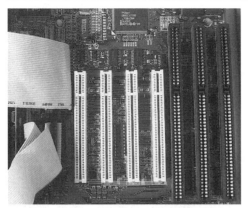

Figure 7.22 Remove the adapter cards from your motherboard.

Figure 7.23 Disconnect the ribbon cables from your attached disk drives.

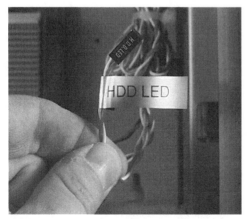

Figure 7.24 Tape labels on the LED connectors that lead to the lights on the front of your PC. This way you'll know what goes where later.

before you remove anything. Make sure you don't lose any screws from the adapter cards.

Keep track of all cables and connectors, since you will be re-assembling them later. Leave the cables plugged into either the adapter cards or the devices they connect to so that you have at least one end in the right place. Use sticky-notes to label all of the cables and wires that you disconnect.

7. Disconnect and remove the ribbon cables attached to the disk drives and motherboard drive connectors, as in **Figure 7.23**.

8. Disconnect the ribbon cables for the serial ports, parallel (printer) port, and mouse port, if these exist.

9. The computer case usually has some LEDs and switches on the front. These are controlled by small connector leads that attach directly to the motherboard from the inside front of the case. These leads are usually labeled, however obscurely, so that you can reconnect them to your new motherboard. Tape labels onto each one (**Figure 7.24**) if they do not already have a marking.

You can determine which lead is which by consulting the documentation for your existing motherboard; it should tell you which connector is attached to which jumper.

The connectors for the case usually include the system power indicator, keyboard lock, turbo switch, turbo indicator, reset switch, speaker, and hard-drive activity indicator. Your motherboard and case may have some or all of these—or even additional leads—but these are the most common.

10. Disconnect the power from the motherboard (**Figure 7.25**).

The motherboard gets power through two leads from the power supply. These leads usually look like one long, thin plug that fits into a power connector on the board, but there are actually two halves. Note that the black wires from each of the power leads are closest to each other. This is the most important point to remember when re-assembling your system—and we will take every opportunity to remind you of it.

11. You should also disconnect the power lead attached to your CPU fan if you have one (**Figure 7.26**).

Some ATX motherboards also provide power to chassis fans; these should be disconnected at this point.

There now should be no connections between your motherboard and the rest of your computer except for the screws and mounting posts holding it in position.

12. Check your case and determine how the motherboard can be physically removed from the system. In some cases you will need to remove a side panel and slide the whole motherboard out, but in most systems you must remove all the screws and slide the board about an inch toward the top or bottom of the case to unclip the mounting posts (**Figure 7.27**).

In some cases, you won't be able to remove the motherboard until you remove the drive bays and other structures inside the case. If you cannot easily slide and rotate your motherboard out of the case once it is unattached, then you may have to start disassembling the rest of the case. Take pictures of each case component that you remove before removing it, or if you do not have a camera, then a quick sketch of the case interior may be a great help.

Figure 7.25 Disconnect the power from the motherboard.

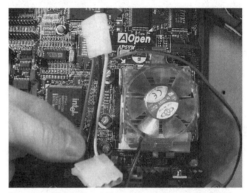

Figure 7.26 Disconnect the power lead from the CPU fan.

Figure 7.27 Unclip the mounting posts.

UPGRADING THE MOTHERBOARD

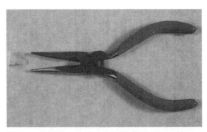

Figure 7.28 Note where the white mounting posts are attached.

Figure 7.29 Attach your new CPU to your motherboard.

Figure 7.30 This is a heat sink fan.

Figure 7.31 Install the RAM on the new motherboard.

When you have the motherboard completely removed from the case, you are ready to get down to the real business of upgrading.

13. If your motherboard is still attached to a removable panel from the side of the case, detach it now. Remove the white mounting posts from the current motherboard and take note of where they were attached (**Figure 7.28**)—they will be reused in the same places for your new motherboard.

Preparing the new board

1. Attach the new CPU to the new motherboard (**Figure 7.29**).

You should also attach the heat sink and heat sink fan, if provided. All CPUs from Pentiums on up should have at least a heat sink attached, with some kind of airflow over the heat sink—a heat sink fan (**Figure 7.30**) is well worth the price.

2. Install the RAM modules on the new motherboard (**Figure 7.31**).

If you are using the memory from your old motherboard, you can remove it from the old board and reinstall it in the new one. You should double-check the documentation for the new motherboard to make sure you are adding the memory to the correct RAM slots if you are not using them all. Remember: For Pentium systems SIMMs must be populated in pairs. EDO RAM does not work in 486 systems. And DIMMs must be rated to work at the speed your system bus is set for.

Note: The order in which you do the preceding two steps doesn't matter, some motherboard documentation may list them in a different sequence.

Installing the new board

1. Once the new motherboard is mounted in the case, you may have difficulty accessing the small components attached directly to it, such as RAM and the CPU, so make sure you have double-checked everything in the previous section before continuing.

   The installation process is pretty much just the reverse of the removal process, but some important points should be heeded, so read through all the steps carefully.

   It is important that the motherboard is firmly supported. Make sure to have mounting posts or threaded posts for screws under the expansion slots on the motherboard because you will be pushing and pulling adapter cards against this area of the board.

2. The new motherboard should mount into your case the same way that the old one did. Insert the mounting posts into the same locations for the new motherboard (**Figure 7.32**).

   In most computer cases the mounting posts will fit into gaps in the mounting panel, and then the whole board will slide about an inch to secure the mounting posts. The holes for the screws should line up over the threaded posts below the motherboard, as in **Figure 7.33**. Secure the new motherboard with at least two screws.

   Use a pair of needle-nosed pliers to remove the mounting posts from the holes in the old motherboard.

3. With the new board correctly fitted into position, connect the power leads from the power supply (**Figure 7.34**).

   As we mentioned previously, the power leads are two identical plugs that fit side-by-side into the power socket on the motherboard, and the black wires on

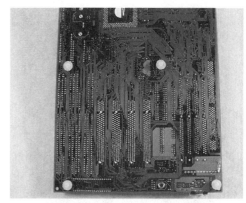

Figure 7.32 Insert the mounting posts on your new motherboard.

Figure 7.33 Line up the screw holes with the threaded posts below the motherboard.

Figure 7.34 Connect the power leads to the motherboard.

Figure 7.35 Connect the CPU fan power lead.

Figure 7.36 Connect the leads that power the lights and buttons on the front of the case.

each plug *must* be next to each other. Your motherboard can burn out very quickly if this connection is not made correctly. The power leads can only be aligned one way in their sockets. The power sockets on an ATX motherboard will only fit power leads from an ATX power supply, and likewise for AT motherboards and power supplies.

4. If your CPU includes a fan, connect the power lead now (**Figure 7.35**).

   The CPU fan/heat sink fan for processors on AT motherboards should plug into one of the power leads for peripherals coming from the power supply. The CPU fan for ATX motherboards should connect to a set of posts on the motherboard. Check your documentation for the correct location of the CPU fan connector.

5. Connect the case connector leads next (**Figure 7.36**).

   If you were diligent about marking each lead, you should have no problem finding the proper lead for each connector documented in the motherboard manual. If the leads from your case are not labeled, and you are not able to mark them, you'll have to follow the wires from each lead to try to find the switch or LED on the front of your case that each operates.

   In some cases, the size of the lead does not match the motherboard connector it is meant to attach to. For Pentium and later motherboards the only connector that is really necessary is the reset switch connector. The PC will still operate normally even if the other leads are disconnected, but you will suffer the inconvenience of not being able to see when your power is turned on or when the hard drive is being accessed. You can usually find the proper place for each connector if you are patient and persistent enough, so don't give up easily!

6. Connect the drive connectors on the motherboard to the cable to the drive(s) in your system.

If you had to remove any of the disk drives from your system to access the motherboard, replace them now (**Figure 7.37**).

If you have an EIDE CD-ROM or DVD-ROM drive, you should connect these devices to the second EIDE controller on the board while the hard disk(s) use the first controller.

Figure 7.37 Replace the hard drives you may have removed.

7. Connect the floppy drives to the floppy-drive controller on the motherboard (**Figure 7.38**).

Note that the floppy drive ribbon cable will have a section where some of the wires twist and the rest remain parallel. This twist should separate the A: and B: floppy drives (if you are installing two floppy drives). The floppy drive that is on the far side of the twist from the controller end will be drive A:, the drive on the same side of the twist as the controller will be drive B:.

Figure 7.38 Connect the floppy drives to the floppy-drive controller.

8. Make the connectors for two serial ports, one parallel port, and in some systems a mouse port (**Figure 7.39**).

Some cases provide two serial ports mounted on the back of the case, and some only provide one, requiring you to add a serial connector in one of the slot covers at the back. ATX systems feature all of these connectors on a panel on the back of the case that is attached to the motherboard.

Figure 7.39 Connect the serial, parallel, and mouse ports.

9. Reinstall all of the adapter cards that you removed from your system and intend to use again (**Figure 7.40**). If you need to upgrade your video card, you should install the new one at this point.

10. Most systems will include a sound card—remember to connect the CD audio

Figure 7.40 Reinstall the adapter cards onto the motherboard.

Figure 7.41 Connect the audio cable to your CD/DVD drive.

```
PNP OS Installed     : Yes        DMA  1 Used By ISA : No/ICU
Slot 1 IRQ           : Auto       DMA  3 Used By ISA : No/ICU
Slot 2 IRQ           : Auto       DMA  5 Used By ISA : No/ICU
Slot 3 IRQ           : Auto
Slot 4 IRQ           : Auto       ISA MEM Block BASE : No/ICU
PCI Latency Timer : 32 PCI Clock
                                  SYMBIOS SCSI BIOS  : Auto
                                  USB IRQ            : Enabled
IRQ  3 Used By ISA : No/ICU       VGA BIOS Sequence  : PCI/AGP
IRQ  4 Used By ISA : No/ICU
IRQ  5 Used By ISA : No/ICU
IRQ  7 Used By ISA : No/ICU
IRQ  9 Used By ISA : No/ICU
IRQ 10 Used By ISA : No/ICU
IRQ 11 Used By ISA : No/ICU
IRQ 12 Used By ISA : No/ICU       ESC : Quit          ↑↓→← : Select Item
IRQ 14 Used By ISA : No/ICU       F1  : Help          PU/PD/+/- : Modify
IRQ 15 Used By ISA : No/ICU       F5  : Old Values    (Shift)F2 : Color
                                  F6  : Load BIOS  Defaults
                                  F7  : Load Setup Defaults
```

Figure 7.42 Check out the system resources in the BIOS menu to ensure they are allocated correctly.

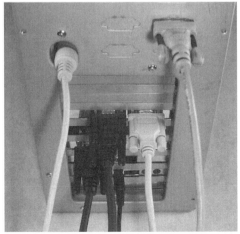

Figure 7.43 Reconnect the power, keyboard, mouse, and monitor cables to the back of your machine.

cable from the CD-ROM or DVD-ROM drive to the sound card (**Figure 7.41**)

11. If you are installing PCI adapter cards, you may have to configure their resources in the BIOS menu of your new motherboard (**Figure 7.42**).

In most cases, the default PCI slot configuration is fine, but if you are using non-Plug N Play ISA adapter cards, you may have an interrupt conflict.

12. Reconnect all of the external connectors such as the power cord, keyboard, mouse, monitor, and printer (**Figure 7.43**).

Leave the computer case open since you stand a pretty good chance of having to correct at least one mistake—no matter how many times you've done this procedure, you always seem to miss a hard-drive LED connector or a floppy-drive cable. At least, *we* do.

13. At last; the moment of truth. Keep one eye on the inside of your case and the other on the monitor, and switch the computer on. Watch for:

The CPU fan and power supply fan should start to spin right away.

After a few seconds the computer should beep. Some motherboards do not make an audible signal when turned on, so don't worry yet. Also, if you missed the internal speaker connector you won't hear anything.

The POST screen should appear after a few seconds and the correct CPU, CPU voltage, and CPU speed should be indicated. Every BIOS displays this information differently and in a different order, but you should see basic system information during the startup sequence like processor type and memory capacity.

The memory total should be displayed and should match the amount you have installed.

Invoke the BIOS setup menu at this point. A quick BIOS recap: Most motherboards allow you to enter the BIOS Setup menu by hitting the Del key (or some other key or combination of keys) during the first part of the boot procedure.

If you do not see instructions on the screen for entering the BIOS Setup menu within a few seconds of turning on the power, then shut off the power and check your documentation. Do not let the operating system attempt to load because you have not configured the hard drive(s) in the BIOS on your new motherboard yet. Some BIOSes will automatically detect hard-disk drives, even if none is configured, but many will not. Whether or not your motherboard can do this, go into the BIOS menu and double check the settings (**Figure 7.44**).

14. After making any necessary changes to the BIOS settings, save them and reboot the machine.

    If you are using the same hard drive you had before the motherboard upgrade, then your operating system should start. Windows 95/98 will start to detect new motherboard devices (**Figure 7.45**) and may need one or two reboots to finally make itself happy with your new hardware.

If the events described above occurred without mishap, then you have successfully replaced your motherboard—congratulations!

If your system does not boot properly, read on for help in investigating the problem.

Troubleshooting after installation

1. If there was no information shown on the display at all, check the monitor power cord and signal connector.

2. If the system beeps several times but shows nothing on the monitor, the video card may not be properly seated.

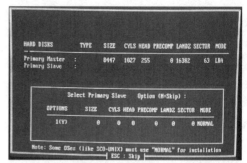

Figure 7.44 Configure your hard-disk controllers in the BIOS.

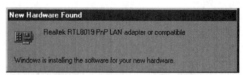

Figure 7.45 After you reboot in Windows, you'll see the Detect New Hardware dialog box. Follow the instructions until Windows is reconfigured.

3. The system may not recognize the RAM installed, the RAM may have been damaged by a static discharge, or the RAM may not be seated correctly. Also, make sure that you have connected the motherboard power leads to the motherboard correctly.

4. If there is an error message describing an "HDD controller failure" or "Hard Disk Error" or something similar, then the hard-disk ribbon cable is probably reversed at one end. Likewise, if the LED on the floppy drive stays on all the time then the floppy-drive ribbon cable is probably reversed at one end.

5. If the computer claims there is no boot device, or if it cannot find the C: drive, then the power lead may have been left off of the hard drive, or the drive is not being correctly detected by the motherboard. You should configure the drive manually in the BIOS setup menu. See Chapter 4 for more information about setting up disk drives.

6. If the hard-disk activity indicator LED does not come on when the disk is in use, then the connector is probably reversed or not connected. Likewise for the turbo and power indicator.

7. Any problem with one component can sometimes be traced to a reversed connection or forgotten power lead for that component. As always, leave the case cover off until you are quite certain all is working properly.

Motherboard compatibilities

The RAM in your current motherboard may not be compatible with the RAM slots in the new motherboard, so you may have to trade-in or buy new RAM. Some motherboards support more than one kind of RAM but you won't get maximum performance from your

UPGRADING THE MOTHERBOARD

new components unless you are using the newest type of RAM that your system supports. If cost is a major concern, then the old RAM can be used until upgrading is more affordable, but you should still check to see what type of RAM you have and what type of RAM your new motherboard can use.

If you are upgrading an older system, you may need to upgrade the video card to work with your new motherboard. If you currently own a 486-class computer, it likely uses a VESA local bus video card. New motherboards use PCI or AGP video cards and cannot use your old VESA hardware.

Some motherboards include built-in video hardware. If your old one did, and your new one doesn't, then you will have to buy a video card.

If you have a really old computer (386 or older), then you probably have an ISA video card. This will still work with newer motherboards, provided they have ISA slots, but the performance of the video card will be abysmal. Note that many PC manufacturers are planning to drop ISA slots from their systems completely within a year or so.

Cheap systems

Recent pricing for new computer systems has gone so low that it is difficult to justify replacing a motherboard just to save money. Most systems will require new RAM, a new video card, and many hours of labor in order to swap motherboards. By the time you add up the costs, it is not much cheaper (and sometimes it's even more expensive) than buying a low-cost PC.

As we mentioned at the beginning of this section, this procedure is meant for those enthusiasts who wish to learn more or who can't stand to see a computer system go to waste.

HARDWARE
RESOURCES

This appendix provides you with common hardware interrupt request (IRQ) and COM port information to help you troubleshoot new installations. It also includes a list of suggested hardware utilities and some helpful Web sites you can visit when you need more information.

Hardware Reference

A physical device in a PC may interrupt the central processing unit in order to exchange or process information. The system checks each device once every fixed period of time to see if it has any information to be processed. Since the system does not know which physical devices are present (the hardware configuration of a PC is very changeable), it relies on each device to use a unique interrupt request address known as an IRQ. The system simply checks each address in sequence when the interrupt cycle occurs. PCs are limited to sixteen hardware IRQs.

If two or more hardware devices try to use the same IRQ, the system cannot communicate with those devices concurrently. So it is important to use a unique IRQ for every hardware device in the computer that requires one.

Who needs IRQs?

Some hardware devices do not appear to need an IRQ. Disk drives, printers, and display monitors do not require you to select an IRQ for them when they are added to the system. However, these devices stille are indirectly using IRQs because they are attached to other devices that have interrupt request addresses. For example, disk drives connect to a drive controller that uses an IRQ, printers connect to the parallel port which uses an IRQ, and a monitor connects to a video display adapter card that uses an IRQ.

There *are* hardware devices that do not require an IRQ and do not attach to any other device that does. Some 3D accelerator add-in cards, for instance, use direct memory access (DMA), bus mastering, or other techniques to communicate directly with system memory or other system components without involving the CPU. But such devices are the exceptions to the general rule that each device requires an IRQ.

Table A.1

Common IRQ Assignments	
TIRQ	DEVICE
0	System timer.
1	Keyboard.
2	Interrupt controller.
3	COM 2 / 4: communication/serial port 2. If you install an internal modem on COM2, you must disable the COM2 device on your motherboard or I/O card.
4	COM 1 / 3: communication/serial port 1. If you install an internal modem on COM1 you must disable the COM1 device on your motherboard or I/O card.
5	LPT 2: printer/parallel port 2 (if present). Usually used for a sound card since most PCs do not have two printer ports.
6	Floppy drive controller.
7	LPT 1: printer/parallel port 1.
8	Real time clock (BIOS clock).
9	Redirected IRQ2 (available to some adapter cards).
10	Available. Network interface cards and SCSI controllers are good devices to put here.
11	Available. Network interface cards and SCSI controllers are good devices to put here.
12	PS/2 mouse port (if present). If your computer does not have a PS/2 style mouse port then this IRQ is available.
13	FPU: math coprocessor.
14	IDE 1: hard disk drive controller 1.
15	IDE 2: hard disk drive controller 2 (if present).

Before the Plug N Play standard became ubiquitous there was a common way to assign IRQ addresses to system devices. If you are working on an older system that does not support plug and play, or have disabled it for any reason, the following IRQ map may be useful. Please note that the assignments in **Table A.1** are common but not universal; always check your PC to verify IRQ assignments before proceeding.

As you will see, few IRQ numbers are available. To add to the difficulty, many ISA adapter cards can only use certain IRQ addresses.

COM ports

Serial ports allow you to communicate with a certain type of hardware known as a *serial* device: modems, for example, and certain printers. Two physical serial devices are available for use in your PC as serial ports, and two more devices may be added. These devices are assigned to one of four logical communication ports: COM1, COM2, COM3, or COM4. However, only two IRQs are available for serial devices, so COM1 and COM3 use the same interrupt but different I/O addresses, and likewise for COM2 and COM4. Confused? The important thing to know is that you can install up to four serial devices on your system, but only two of them can be accessed at a time.

For example: If you install a modem on COM1 and a serial mouse on COM2 then you have used both available serial device IRQs in your computer. If you then want to add a null-modem cable or a serial printer to your system you have to enable a serial port on either COM3 or COM4. But if you use COM3 then the modem on COM1 will not work while you access the null-modem cable or serial printer. On the other hand, if you use COM4 then the mouse on COM2 will not work while you use the device on COM4.

(Obviously, it is preferable to use the COM port that does not disable the mouse, because it is tricky to navigate most applications without it.)

Standard IRQ and I/O mappings for serial ports can be found in **Table A.2**. Once again, these are fairly common, but the mappings for your PC may be different.

In some BIOS documentation, a COM port is only referred to by its I/O address, so Table A.2 may be able to help you determine the proper address to use.

Table A.2

Common COM port addresses

IRQ	COM
3	COM2 or COM4
4	COM1 or COM3

COM	I/O Addresses
1	3F8
2	2F8
3	3E8
4	2E8

Hardware Utilities

Unless you are working on a PC that you have previously configured yourself, many of the IRQ assignments may be unknown to you. Although you can figure out quite a bit by opening the case and looking at the adapter card settings, some utilities are available that make this unnecessary. Here is a list of some of the best and easiest programs you should try.

SiSoft Sandra98

This utility comes in two versions: a free Standard version, and an enhanced Professional version. Even the Standard version is amazingly full-featured and includes windows that help you identify physical and logical system components, system software, hardware IRQs, benchmarks for CPUs and disks, and many other attributes of your computer.

The Professional version adds windows for I/O addresses, power consumption features, CMOS, BIOS information, and much more.

The Sandra98 utility is highly recommended for querying system information that is otherwise difficult to find, like video card memory capacity and IRQ settings. You can find the latest version of Sandra98 on the Web at:

http://www.sisoftware.demon.co.uk/sandra/

Microsoft Diagnostics

The Microsoft Diagnostics (MSD) utility is a small DOS program that was included with version 6.x of MS-DOS and many iterations of Windows 3.x. Though it works quite well under Windows 95 and 98, it is not included with those operating systems, so finding a copy of it can be a little bit difficult these days.

MSD includes screens that list the hardware IRQs, COM ports, LPT ports, disk drives, and a few other system devices. It should be run in DOS mode and *not* in a DOS session under Windows. MSD is quite handy for working on machines that do not have Windows installed.

Winfiles.com

This is a good Web site with a comprehensive collection of Windows software. The system diagnostics section is quite large and can be found at:

http://www.winfiles.com/apps/98/system-analyze.html

Hardware Resources on the Web

Here is a list of some of our favorite places on the Internet to find out about PC hardware.

Tom's Hardware

This site is run by a German medical student who, if he knows as much about medicine as he does about computer hardware, will someday be the world's best doctor. There is a collection of articles explaining and comparing just about every hardware device that you would find inside a PC, making this is a great starting point for those who want to know more about PCs. The site is renowned for its bad grammar and flawless technical detail.

http://www.tomshardware.com/

Maximum PC

This magazine-style Web site caters to the savvy, upscale PC user. In addition to news and reviews, there is a question and answer forum that deals with those sticky hardware issues that no one else can resolve. Don't miss the section called "Ask the Saint," written by an ex-Microsoft bigwig whose opinionated predictions are justified by their uncanny accuracy.

http://www.maximumpc.com/

C/Net's Gamecenter.com

Though this site is dedicated to computer games, it frequently runs articles about what's new in the PC hardware world. Because gamers are some of the most demanding hardware connoisseurs, anyone looking for good reviews for video cards and other hardware should surf here.

http://www.gamecenter.com/

Gamespot.com

Not only does this Web site often post reviews of computer hardware, it also runs how-to articles and comparea hardware for budget-conscious buyers in the hardware section.

http://www.gamespot.com/

OEM Web sites

Your best bet for resolving problems with specific devices is to visit the manufacturers' home pages on the Internet. Finding the home page is usually pretty simple: Look in the documentation for your device for a Web site address or do a search on a search engine such as Yahoo (www.yahoo.com) for the hardware company's name.

There are occasions when these paths do not lead you to the proper Web site, though. If the problematic hardware is very old, or if the manufacturer is obscure, out of business, or has been taken over by another company, then the name of the original company may not show up anywhere. In those cases, you can continue your searching at DejaNews (www.dejanews.com).

This search will look through the archive of Usenet postings for your search term. As long as you are not the only person in the world that bought the device, chances are that someone else has been asking about it on the Usenet.

If your searching still fails to find the answers you need, then you could post a question on Usenet. Use the DejaNews posting form if you are not familiar with how to post messages in Usenet newsgroups:

http://www.dejanews.com/post.xp

This form will also help you find the proper newsgroup in which to post your question. Hopefully, someone there can help you solve your hardware problem!

CPU
UPGRADE TABLE

The following table lists the CPU processors commonly available over the past five years, the socket type or motherboard chipset on the motherboard, and the potentially fastest processor upgrade available without changing the motherboard. Note that this information is current at the time of writing, but you should check the Intel, AMD, and Cyrix Web sites for the most recent information.

The Recommended column indicates if we feel that this upgrade is worth the time and trouble, but does not account for the cost, as processor prices are continuously declining as faster models become available. When no upgrade is recommended, then that means it may be time to go shopping for a new PC. Note: There are no Intel Overdrive or alternative upgrade processors available for Pentium II systems.

CPU Upgrade Table

CPU	MOTHERBOARD CHIPSET OR SOCKET TYPE	UPGRADE AVAILABLE: 1. INTEL STANDARD PROCESSOR 2. INTEL OVERDRIVE PROCESSOR 3. AMD PROCESSOR UPGRADE 4. CYRIX OR OTHER PROCESSOR UPGRADE	RECOMMENDED?
486 33 MHz	N/A	486 10 [1,2]	Yes
		486-66 Overdrive [2]	Yes
		AMD 486DX4-100 / AMD 5x86-100/133	Yes / Yes
		Cyrix 486DX22 / 5x86 [2]	No / Yes
486 50	N/A	486 100 [1,2]	Yes
		486-100 Overdrive [2]	Yes
		AMD 486DX4-100 / AMD 5x86-100/133	Yes / Yes
		Cyrix 486DX22 / 5x86 [2]	No / Yes
486 66	N/A	486 100 [1,2]	Yes
		486-100 Overdrive [2]	Yes
		AMD 486DX4-100 / AMD 5x86-100/133	Yes / Yes
		Cyrix 5x86 [2]	Yes
486 100	N/A	486 100 [1,2]	No
		486-100 Overdrive [2]	No
		AMD 5x86-100/133	Yes
		Cyrix 5x86 [2]	Yes
Pentium 60	Socket 4	Pentium 66 [2]	No
		Pentium Overdrive [2]	No
		AMD K6 MMX 266 [2,3]	Yes
		Cyrix 6x86MX MMX 233 or 266 [2,3]	Yes
Pentium 66	Socket 4	Pentium 66 [2]	No
		Pentium Overdrive [2]	No
		AMD K6 MMX 266 [2,3]	Yes
		Cyrix 6x86MX MMX 233 or 266 [2,3]	Yes
Pentium 75	Socket 5	Pentium 166 [1]	Yes
		Pentium Overdrive 150 MMX	Yes
		AMD K6 MMX 266 or AMD K6-2	Yes
		Evergreen MxPro 180 or 200	Yes

[1] You must consult your motherboard documentation or contact your system vendor to find out the maximum processor speed that your system will support. The processor shown in this table indicates the best-case upgrade, but not all motherboards will support this. Also, many older motherboards will not support Intel CPUs with MMX technology.

[2] This processor is discontinued but may still be available from third-party vendors.

[3] Third-party products are available to make this processor work in this type of CPU socket.

[4] Most Intel BX motherboards will need the newest BIOS installed before they can support the Pentium III CPU. Contact your computer or motherboard vendor for BIOS information and upgrades.

CPU Upgrade Table *(continued)*

CPU	MOTHERBOARD CHIPSET OR SOCKET TYPE	UPGRADE AVAILABLE: 1. INTEL STANDARD PROCESSOR 2. INTEL OVERDRIVE PROCESSOR 3. AMD PROCESSOR UPGRADE 4. CYRIX OR OTHER PROCESSOR UPGRADE	RECOMMENDED?
Pentium 75	Socket 7	Pentium 233 MMX[1]	Yes
		Pentium Overdrive 150 MMX	Yes
		AMD K6 MMX 266 / AMD K6-2	Yes / Yes
		Cyrix M II / Evergreen MxPro 180 or 200	Yes / Yes
Pentium 90	Socket 5	Pentium 166[1]	No
		Pentium Overdrive 180 MMX	Yes
		AMD K6 MMX 266 / AMD K6-2	Yes / Yes
		Evergreen MxPro 180 or 200	Yes
Pentium 90	Socket 7	Pentium 233 MMX[1]	Yes
		Pentium Overdrive 180 MMX	Yes
		AMD K6 MMX 266 / AMD K6-2	Yes / Yes
		Cyrix M II / Evergreen MxPro 180 or 200	Yes / Yes
Pentium 100	Socket 5	Pentium 166[1]	No
		Pentium Overdrive 166 MMX	No
		AMD K6 MMX 266 / AMD K6-2	Yes / Yes
		Evergreen MxPro 180 or 200	Yes / Yes
Pentium 100	Socket 7	Pentium 233 MMX[1]	Yes
		Pentium Overdrive 200 MMX	Yes
		AMD K6 MMX 266 / AMD K6-2	Yes / Yes
		Cyrix M II / Evergreen MxPro 180 or 200	Yes / Yes
Pentium 120	Socket 5	Pentium 166[1]	No
		Pentium Overdrive 180 MMX	No
		AMD K6 MMX 266 / AMD K6-2	Yes / Yes
		Evergreen MxPro 180 or 200	Yes
Pentium 120	Socket 7	Pentium 233 MMX[1]	No
		Pentium Overdrive 180 MMX	No
		AMD K6 MMX 266 / AMD K6-2	Yes / Yes
		Cyrix M II / Evergreen MxPro 180 or 200	Yes / No
Pentium 133	Socket 5	Pentium 166[1]	No
		Pentium Overdrive 166 MMX	No
		AMD K6 MMX 266 / AMD K6-2	Yes / Yes
		Evergreen MxPro 180 or 200	Yes
Pentium 133	Socket 7	Pentium 233 MMX[1]	No
		Pentium Overdrive 200 MMX	No
		AMD K6 MMX 266 or AMD K6-2	Yes / Yes
		Cyrix M II / Evergreen MxPro 180 or 200	Yes / No

CPU UPGRADE TABLE

CPU Upgrade Table *(continued)*

CPU	MOTHERBOARD CHIPSET OR SOCKET TYPE	UPGRADE AVAILABLE: 1. INTEL STANDARD PROCESSOR 2. INTEL OVERDRIVE PROCESSOR 3. AMD PROCESSOR UPGRADE 4. CYRIX OR OTHER PROCESSOR UPGRADE	RECOMMENDED?
Pentium 150	Socket 5	Pentium 166 [1]	No
		Pentium Overdrive 180 MMX	No
		AMD K6 MMX 266 / AMD K6-2	No / Yes
		Evergreen MxPro 180 or 200	No
Pentium 150	Socket 7	Pentium 233 MMX [1]	No
		Pentium Overdrive 180 MMX	No
		AMD K6 MMX 266 / AMD K6-2	No / Yes
		Cyrix M II / Evergreen MxPro 180 or 200	Yes / No
Pentium 166	Socket 5	Pentium 166 [1]	No
		Pentium Overdrive 166 MMX	No
		AMD K6 MMX 266 / AMD K6-2	No / Yes
		Evergreen MxPro 180 or 200	Yes / No
Pentium 166	Socket 7	Pentium 233 MMX [1]	No
		Pentium Overdrive 200 MMX	No
		AMD K6 MMX 266 / AMD K6-2	No / Yes
		Cyrix M II / Evergreen MxPro 180 or 200	Yes / No
Pentium 166 MMX	Socket 7	Pentium 233 MMX [1]	No
		Pentium Overdrive 200 MMX	No
		AMD K6 MMX 266 / AMD K6-2	No / Yes
		Cyrix M II / Evergreen MxPro 180 or 200	Yes / No
Pentium 200	Socket 7	Pentium 233 MMX [1]	No
		Pentium Overdrive 200 MMX	No
		AMD K6 MMX 266 / AMD K6-2	No / No
		Cyrix M II / Evergreen MxPro 200	No / No
Pentium 200 MMX	Socket 7	Pentium 233 MMX [1]	No
		None available	N/A
		AMD K6 MMX 266 / AMD K6-2	No / No
		Cyrix M II / Evergreen MxPro 200	No / No

CPU UPGRADE TABLE

[1] You must consult your motherboard documentation or contact your system vendor to find out the maximum processor speed that your system will support. The processor shown in this table indicates the best-case upgrade, but not all motherboards will support this. Also, many older motherboards will not support Intel CPUs with MMX technology.

[2] This processor is discontinued but may still be available from third-party vendors.

[3] Third-party products are available to make this processor work in this type of CPU socket.

[4] Most Intel BX motherboards will need the newest BIOS installed before they can support the Pentium III CPU. Contact your computer or motherboard vendor for BIOS information and upgrades.

CPU Upgrade Table *(continued)*

CPU	MOTHERBOARD CHIPSET OR SOCKET TYPE	UPGRADE AVAILABLE: 1. INTEL STANDARD PROCESSOR 2. INTEL OVERDRIVE PROCESSOR 3. AMD PROCESSOR UPGRADE 4. CYRIX OR OTHER PROCESSOR UPGRADE	RECOMMENDED?
Pentium 233 MMX	Socket 7	Pentium 233 MMX	No
		None available	N/A
		AMD K6 MMX 266 / AMD K6-2	No / No
		Cyrix M II / Evergreen MxPro 200	No / No
Pentium Pro 150	Socket 8	Pentium Pro 200	No
		Overdrive: Pentium II 300	Yes
		None available	N/A
		None available	N/A
Pentium Pro 166	Socket 8	Pentium Pro 200	No
		Overdrive: Pentium II 333	Yes
		None available	N/A
		None available	N/A
Pentium Pro 180	Socket 8	Pentium Pro 200	No
		Overdrive: Pentium II 300	Yes
		None available	N/A
		None available	N/A
Pentium Pro 200	Socket 8	Pentium Pro 200	No
		Overdrive: Pentium II 333	No
		None available	N/A
		None available	N/A
Pentium II 233	Intel LX	Pentium II 333	No
Pentium II 233	Intel BX	Pentium III 500A	Yes
Pentium II 266	Intel LX	Pentium II 333	No
Pentium II 266	Intel BX	Pentium III 500A	Yes
Pentium II 300	Intel LX	Pentium II 333	No
Pentium II 300	Intel BX	Pentium III 500A	Yes
Pentium II 333	Intel LX	Pentium II 333	No
Pentium II 333	Intel BX	Pentium III 500A	No
Pentium II 350	Intel BX	Pentium III 500A	No
Pentium II 400	Intel BX	Pentium III 500A	No
Pentium II 450	Intel BX	Pentium III 500A	No
Pentium III 450	Intel BX	Pentium III 500A	No
Pentium III 500	Intel BX	Pentium III 500	No

GLOSSARY

3D graphics accelerators

The newest generation of video cards have special microprocessors built into them that can draw and rotate "three-dimensional" images on your two-dimensional monitor much faster than your PC's CPU. These cards improve performance if software is written to take advantage of them.

386

The first 32-bit CPU for personal computers, released by Intel in 1986. Intel is the company that develops most of the new technology that goes into PCs.

486

The second generation 32-bit microprocessor made for PCs. The 486 runs faster than most 386s, which means, of course, better performance.

AGP (Accelerated Graphics Port)

This special high-speed motherboard slot is designed to accommodate video boards that display 3D images faster.

AMD

A manufacturer that produces CPU chips.

application

A program, like Microsoft Word or a game, that runs on your computer.

auto-detect

Windows 95/98 will usually notice that new hardware has been installed and prompt you to identify and supply the correct drivers for the hardware in question.

AUTOEXEC.BAT

A text file that runs automatically as soon as DOS has started. It usually tells your computer to load more device drivers or other utilities.

backup

A backup involves making safety copies of the files on your hard drive to another piece of media (floppy, CD-ROM, tape drive) in order to have redundant copies available if the original files become damaged or deleted.

BIOS (Basic Input/Output System)

The BIOS is code that's built into a ROM chip on your computer's motherboard. This chip tells the PC how to load the operating system and how to access hardware devices like the hard drive and video card.

boot

Refers to the way the BIOS loads the operating system each time the computer is turned on. Turning on a computer is called *booting* it.

boot disk

A disk that contains enough pieces of an operating system that it is capable of starting your computer. May be a hard disk or a floppy diskette.

cache

(Pronounced like *cash*.) A temporary data storage location in memory. By temporarily caching information from the hard disk in memory, the computer can access it faster. Likewise, memory can be cached on a hard drive file as well.

CD-ROM (Compact Disc Read Only Memory)

Optical disks that look like music CDs, can store about 650 MB of data, and are far less sensitive to damage than a hard drive. However, CD-ROMs are just that, read-only, and ordinary CD-ROM drives can only read data; they can't write it.

clock speed

The speed at which your processor runs, measured in MHz (millions of pulses per second). The higher the number, the faster the clock speed.

color depth

Refers to the number of colors that a video card can display. The color depth that a video card is capable at any given screen resolution is dependent on the amount of memory on the video card.

CONFIG.SYS

A file that DOS reads to determine how to configure memory and load device drivers. Usually unnecessary with Windows 95/98.

Control Panel

The Control Panel is a window containing a number of utility icons used to set basic Windows defaults and report configuration information. An example of a Control Panel utility is the one you use to set date and time. You can access the Control Panel from the Start Menu.

GLOSSARY

CPU (Central Processing Unit)

This is the so-called brain of your computer, the chip that does most of the actual computing. Varieties include the 80486 (known as 486) and 80586 (known as a Pentium), or Pentium II. CPUs are made by Intel, AMD, and Cyrix, among other companies.

Cyrix

Cyrix, like AMD, produces low-cost CPUs that are compatible with, and compete against, Intel.

default

A setting that will be used automatically unless you change it. A preset value.

dialog box

A window that allows you to interact with the operating system or a computer program. Usually features at least two buttons: OK and Cancel.

DIMM (Dual Inline Memory Module)

DIMM is one type of RAM (Random Access Memory).

DIP switch

A DIP switch is a small toggle switch used to configure a board or peripheral. These switches are often mounted in multiples, and can either be set to 'on' or 'off'.

disk drive

An electro-mechanical device that uses a magnetic platter to store information. Although floppy and CD-ROM drive are disk drives, hard disk drives (or simply hard drives) are usually the kind that is meant by the term *disk drive*. Hard drives store most of your PC's software, including Windows 95/98.

DLL (Dynamic Link Library)

A file with the extension DLL contains code and performs common functions when a particular program is running.

DMA (Direct Memory Access)

DMA is a way for peripherals to access memory without using the CPU. Each peripheral that needs DMA must have its own unique DMA number assigned.

DOS (Disk Operating System)

Introduced in 1982, this is one of the early command-line interfaces (it didn't use a mouse). These days, the only place you're likely to see it is inside a Windows DOS box (although Windows 95 and 98 still contain some DOS code).

download

The process of receiving data from a remote location, whether over the Internet, or via a network.

drive bay

A space inside a computer that's designed to hold a hard drive, a CD-ROM drive, or a floppy drive.

driver

A small program that lets your PC talk to a piece of hardware. The driver is specific to the hardware and the operating system you use. Most new hardware comes with its own set of device drivers.

DVD-ROM (Digital Versatile Disc Read Only Memory)

DVD-ROM is the next step in the evolution of CD-ROM. Theoretically, DVD-ROM discs can store up to 17GB of data each.

EIDE (Enhanced Integrated Drive Electronics)

Currently the most common hard disk interface specification (SCSI is an alternative). The EIDE standard also supports CD-ROMs and some other types of hardware devices.

Ethernet

A kind of network card; also, a network standard by which computers can communicate over a linked series of cables.

format

A predetermined layout in which data can later be stored on media (hard drive, floppy drive). Also the act of creating this layout. Normally, you must format a new hard drive before you can store any data on it.

full backup

A full backup involves making safety copies of all of the files from all your hard drives on a given computer to another medium for safety and redundancy reasons in case the original files are damaged or deleted.

Gigabyte

Approximately one billion bytes.

graphics card

(See **video card**.)

hard drive

The electromagnetic disk drive inside your PC where your computer stores on magnetic platters the operating system and most of the programs you run. Some PCs have more than one hard drive, and some use external hard drives that sit outside the PC in their own cases. Most contemporary hard drives are controlled by EIDE or SCSI standards.

Hertz

Hertz is a measure of frequency defined as one cycle per second. Computer CPUs run in MHz (Megahertz), which is millions of cycles per second.

hot swapping

This refers to the plugging and unplugging of devices from your computer without first turning off the power.

IDE (Integrated Drive Electronics)

Like EIDE or SCSI, IDE is an interface between hard drives, CD-ROMS, and your motherboard.

Input/Output (I/O)

Usually refers to ports (like a serial port) which channel data into and out of the PC.

interrupt

When a peripheral needs to communicate with the CPU, it sends a signal called an interrupt. Each peripheral that uses interrupts must have its own unique interrupt number. Interrupts are set with jumpers on the PC card, or automatically in the case of plug and play devices.

IRQs

See **interrupt**.

jumper

A small metal pin that connects two metal posts on a PC card. Used to change the settings on a PC card or hard drive.

Kilobyte

Approximately one thousand bytes.

LAN (Local Area Network)

A group of computers in relatively close physical proximity that are connected together via a network such as Ethernet.

Megabyte

Approximately one million bytes.

Megahertz

(See **Hertz**.)

Microsoft

The company that developed DOS and Windows, currently by far the most popular operating systems for the PC. Microsoft also produces other top-selling software products such as Word, Excel, and Outlook.

MIDI (Musical Instrument Digital Interface)

MIDI is an interface designed to work with digital synthesizers and musical instruments so that a PC can communicate with them.

modem

A device that allows a PC to exchange data with another computer via a phone line.

monitor

Also commonly called the *display, screen,* or *CRT.* The television-like box on which you watch the results of your computer's work. The image on your monitor comes from the video card, but it's a combination of the entire machine working in unison that brings the images to coherent life on your screen.

Moore's Law

A prophetic prediction by Gordon Moore (a co-founder of Intel) that the number of transistors that could be fit onto a computer chip would double every 18 months.

motherboard

The main circuit board in your PC, holding the CPU, RAM, various adapter cards, and lots of other useful stuff.

multiscan

Multiscan refers to a monitor that can process a video signal at various refresh rates.

NetBeui (NetBIOS Extended User Interface)

A protocol used to connect computers over a newtork.

Netware

A network operating system developed by Novell that's usually used in client-server architecture.

network

A collection of computers connected via a series of network cards and cables that allows them to exchange data.

NIC (Network Interface Card)

A PC card that plugs into your computer and connects it to the local area network.

OEM (Original Equipment Manufacturer)

Computer vendors like Compaq or Dell often include special versions of Windows 98 (and other software) that are customized to work with their equipment. These are called OEM versions because technically they come from the original equipment manufacturer (i.e. Dell), not from the maker of the operating system (i.e. Microsoft).

OS (Operating System)

The master software program that manages your computer and interprets between the hardware and applications.

parallel port

A communications port that sends and receives 8 bits of data at once. All modern PCs have parallel ports, also known as printer ports.

peer-to-peer network

A computer network that allows every workstation to see and access resources on every other workstation.

Pentium/Pentium II/586

Recent CPUs from Intel.

peripheral

A hardware device installed inside or attached to your PC. Examples include hard drives, sound cards, and mice.

pixel (picture element)

One of the numerous glowing dots that your monitor displays. All of the graphics and pictures that the PC draws on the monitor are made up of pixels.

Plug N Play

A standard that attempts to make PCs configure new hardware devices automatically. Ideally, when a Plug N Play card is inserted into the computer, it should simply work without any fuss. For Plug N Play to work right you need a Plug N Play BIOS on your motherboard, a Plug N Play operating system like Windows 95/98 (but not NT), and Plug N Play peripherals.

port

A physical connector through which data enters and leaves a piece of hardware, such as a computer.

power supply

The transformer that converts AC power from the electrical outlet into usable power for your computer.

Processor

(See **CPU**.)

Program Manager

The default shell for Windows 3.1, the master program that allows users to double-click on icons and start applications.

protocol

One of several standard methods that modems and computers use to talk to one another over the Internet, or a LAN.

RAM (Random Access Memory)

The main memory of the PC. Programs load from the hard disk to RAM and are stored there temporarily. Most programs require a minimum amount of RAM in order to operate.

README

A file of last-minute instructions, changes, and information about an application or game that is usually included on the installation disks. The README file is almost always a plain text file that you can view in Notepad, Microsoft Word, or any text editor.

reboot

The act of restarting the computer.

refresh rate

This refers to the number of times the video card and/or the monitor can redraw an image in a given period of time. Usually this measurement is given in Hertz. For example, just about every VGA card will show the 640 x 480 video mode at 60 Hz. Higher refresh rates produce less flicker on your screen.

resolution

The number of pixels shown on a display monitor.

ROM (Read Only Memory)

Memory stored permanently on a chip. ROM memory (like a BIOS chip) or media (such as a CD-ROM) retains stored information even when the power is turned off. The basic operating instructions that let your computer load the operating system are stored in ROM. They are not modifiable by any programs or the operating system.

SCSI (Small Computer System Interface)

Pronounced "scuzzy." SCSI is a high-speed interface standard for your hard drives, CD-ROMs, and other peripherals. Few PCs use it, but all modern Macintosh computers have SCSI built-in.

serial port

A serial port is a connection that sends data in a stream (1 bit at a time) rather than at 8 bits at a time as a parallel port does.

server

The "boss" computer on a network, dedicated to providing resources to other computers on the network. For example: files, printing, or other application services.

SIMMs (Single Inline Memory Modules)

The RAM chips used in most 486s and all older Pentium PCs.

SRAM (Static Random Access Memory)

A kind of fast memory.

swap file

A swap file (also known as a *Virtual Memory File*) is a file on the hard disk that the computer uses to store data temporarily when it runs out of RAM. It allows the computer to load more programs than it actually has room for in memory. However, since disk access is a lot slower than memory access, using a swap file slows down the PC's performance.

throughput

The rate of information transfer between the PC and a peripheral device.

USB (Universal Serial Bus)

A port that allows high speed data transfer as well as such features as hot-swapping and chained connection of over 120 devices on one computer. USB is the wave of the future, and most new machines have USB jacks.

video card

The adapter card that sends images to the monitor via the monitor cable.

video modes

This describes various combinations of resolution, color depth, and refresh rate.

wavetable

A library of sound waves that have been digitized and stored. Wavetable synthesis is a method by which sound cards play MIDI music by using digitized samples taken from actual musical instruments. This results in a more realistic sound than using an FM synthesizer chip.

World Wide Web

This defines all of the resources on the Internet that use the Hypertext Transport Protocol and that can be accessed using Web browsers such as Netscape Communicator and Microsoft Internet Explorer.

Windows 3.1

Microsoft's first successful Graphic User Interface (GUI) operating environment, and the forerunner to Windows 95/98.

Windows 95/98

The current, extremely widely deployed operating system from Microsoft. We put a slash there because Windows 95 and Windows 98 are so similar. Most of the operations discussed in this book that apply to Windows 95 or 98 also apply to the other one as well.

INDEX

INDEX